Trying Home

Trying Home

The Rise and Fall of an Anarchist Utopia on Puget Sound

XOXOX

Justin Wadland

Oregon State University Press
Corvallis

The paper in this book meets the guidelines for permanence and durability of the Committee on Production Guidelines for Book Longevity of the Council on Library Resources and the minimum requirements of the American National Standard for Permanence of Paper for Printed Library Materials Z39.48-1984.

Library of Congress Cataloging-in-Publication Data

Wadland, Justin.
  Trying Home : the rise and fall of an anarchist utopia on Puget Sound / Justin Wadland.
     pages cm
  Includes bibliographical references and index.
  ISBN 978-0-87071-742-0 (paperback) — ISBN 978-0-87071-743-7 (e-book)
1. Home (Wash.)—History. 2. Collective settlements—Washington (State)—History. 3. Utopias—Washington (State)—History. 4. Anarchism—Washington (State)—History. I. Title.
  F899.H66W34 2014
  979.7—dc23

                            2013045029

First published in 2014 by Oregon State University Press
Printed in the United States of America

Oregon State University Press
121 The Valley Library
Corvallis OR 97331-4501
541-737-3166 • fax 541-737-3170
www.osupress.oregonstate.edu

Table of Contents

"Adding salt to the sea, the *Collburnary*, which had that as its cargo, sank off Cameret, Finistère. The crew was rescued."
—Félix Fénéon, *Novels in Three Lines*

"I fully agree that babbling liberally and eloquently is extremely pleasant, while acting is a bit rough."
—Fyodor Dostoyevsky, *Demons*

"Home was like any other place, except for its memories."
—Murray Morgan, *The Last Wilderness*

Introduction

IN THE OLD LEDGER BOOK, the first thirty pages had been torn out long ago. On page thirty-one, a loose cursive with lots of crossings out sprawls across the ruled columns. I flip through the book, disappointed. Except for a few pages, it is blank. Why was it even saved all these years in an archival box at the University of Washington Special Collections?

I'd hoped the ledger might be a diary of sorts, a glimpse of daily life in Home, Washington, during its time as a utopian experiment in anarchism, but Jay Fox wrote these few notes late in life, perhaps in the 1950s. By then, he was an old anarchist who might pull out his ancient printing press and regale a visiting reporter with colorful stories, but he had become a mellow, congenial man of memories. In his notes, Fox reminisces on anarchism and the labor movement, topics to which he had dedicated his life. Then comes the last sentence written in the book, appearing as if a grand finale before hundreds of empty pages: "As an old warrior about to leave the battlefield my prime interest is in the youth who will carry on the struggle and finally bring about the realization of glorious freedom I have so long dreamed of and fought for."[1] The sentence crackles with a kind of prophecy and familiarity, as if I am hearing Jay Fox's own voice aloud in the quiet reading room, and as he often did in life, he speaks for Home.

Jay Fox and his anarchist newspaper, *The Agitator*, are what led me to Home. I first happened upon *The Agitator* over a decade ago, when I was a graduate student at the University of Washington, studying to become a librarian. It was but one of hundreds of small community newspapers I was helping to catalog. My job was to assign genre terms that described the intended audience of the newspapers. When I saw *The Agitator*, snippets of text immediately caught my eye: "*The Agitator* will stand for freedom, first, last and all of the time. It will insist upon the right of every person to express his or her opinion." Or in another column: "*The Agitator* will help banish all of the many varied superstitions handed down from the mystic past as much as its space will permit; but its main object of assault will be the errors surrounding the economic and political life of the people."[2] But some of the other things—references to strikes and political events and long philosophical tracts—I could not place in historical context.

I did some research into *The Agitator* and the town where it was published, and I learned that Home, Washington, was the last and most colorful blossoming of the utopian experiments that found fertile soil in the wilderness around Puget Sound during the late nineteenth century. Organized according to principles of anarchism, individualism, and liberty, the community attracted the attention of radicals across the country, as well as the ire of its more conventionally minded neighbors in surrounding small towns and in the larger city of Tacoma, about fifteen miles due east across the water. Jay Fox moved to Home in 1910, thinking that it might be an affordable place to run a printing press. His newspaper flourished for a while, but Home turned out to not be such a cozy place for Fox and his ideas. Within a year, he would be arrested for an article published in *The Agitator* and brought to trial in Tacoma. Ultimately, his case would be appealed to the United States Supreme Court.

This little community on the soggy fringe of the frontier struggled with many of the principles and ideas that would later be taken up by American society at large. Historian Charles LeWarne writes that it is too simple to say that the people of Home were ahead of their time because by definition radicals must be ahead of their time. Yet he asserts that in their general open-minded tolerance, emphasis on equality of the sexes, civil disobedience, and arguments in favor of free speech, "the individualists of Home were addressing themselves to issues that society would later be forced to confront."[3]

During Home's twenty-five years as a practical experiment in anarchism, residents faced many legal, social, and personal trials. Over the years, an undue amount of litigation complicated the lives of colony members. Various editors, writers, and even the postmistress of Home were hauled in for publishing and distributing materials considered dangerously obscene or insubordinate. Once in court, these anarchists found themselves defending core principles articulated in the United States Constitution, such as the First Amendment guarantee to free speech. Other times they were swept up in cases that made national headlines, such as when Donald Vose, a young man who grew up in Home, turned spy for the Burns Detective Agency and helped track down anarchist fugitives involved in the bombing of the *Los Angeles Times* building. Then when the community could no longer settle its disputes over commonly held land and the management of colony affairs, they were forced to resort to lengthy civil suits.

External forces may have threatened the settlement—such as when the Loyal League in Tacoma sought to wipe out the colony after President McKinley's assassination by an anarchist in 1901—but the ultimate challenge to Home's cohesion and viability came from within. As a community valuing liberty above all else and resolutely averse to coercion in any form, Home was in conflict with itself from the beginning. In the early days, the small group of pioneering founders were too busy sawing down fir trees and building houses to notice any weaknesses, and they could easily dream of Home City becoming a vanguard of civilization. As the years passed, though, and Home became more established, it attracted people who did not share the original vision of the founders. The dissonance between the aspirations of the founders and the all-too-human flaws of the participants demonstrated that the attempt to imagine a new way of life in Home was the biggest trial of all.

It would be trite to say that they failed. By definition, aren't all utopias bound for failure? Hadn't they gotten the memo that "utopia," a term first coined by Sir Thomas More in the sixteenth century, means "no place"? The flaws of the utopian impulse, the stark discord between dream and reality in the attempt to establish an ideal society, are easy to see from the outside, in hindsight. Yet the founders of Home would be the first to point out they were conducting an experiment upon themselves, and the data they collected in their own haphazard way still has relevance today. In *Trying Home*, I sift through the evidence—the newspapers, diaries, first-hand accounts, court transcripts—as a librarian and a storyteller to recreate what it was like to live through the experiment. This story demonstrates that the human organizations we take for granted, from the family unit to the nation-state, are not facts but entities enacted by our own participation in them.

I wish I could say that I fell in with the anarchists of Home purely out of curiosity and admiration of their noble experiment. The name itself drew me to Home for personal reasons that I was not entirely aware of at the outset. While I was growing up, my family moved just enough times that I entered adulthood with questions about the nature of home smoldering in my unconscious: *What is home? Where is home? How will I know when I've found home?* Reconstructing the story of Home made me aware of these questions, then guided me obliquely into and through them. I found along the way that at the heart of any utopian experiment is the deep-seated, human impulse to find and establish an ideal home.

I have lived in Tacoma for eight years, Washington State for thirteen, the longest I have lived anywhere, and I am just now becoming comfortable with calling this place home. Sure, the accumulation of seasons between the snows of Mount Rainier and tides of Puget Sound has had its effect on me. Moss grows easily here, but that's only part of the process. After my wife and I bought our old side-gabled craftsman house, we spent four days stripping wallpaper off the walls and ceilings in the living and dining rooms. It seemed like such a huge chore at the time, one that left us bone tired and sore, but it was the first of many projects we would undertake to cultivate a space for our growing family.

While writing this book, I witnessed the birth of my son, and we are now expecting another. The coincidence of unearthing the story of Home and becoming a parent helped me to recognize that home is not purely a place but something created by care, effort, and sacrifice. For this unexpected lesson, I owe a debt to Home.

CHAPTER ONE
The Mother of Progress Finds Home

IN FEBRUARY 1896, three men with able hands built a small, wooden boat and ventured into south Puget Sound. Beyond their place of departure in Tacoma and their destination—Von Geldern Cove on the Key Peninsula, or Joe's Bay as it was known locally for the man who first settled there—few details remain about the boat or the journey itself. Some accounts mention oars, while others describe a sail. All sources agree that the men who fashioned the boat were dreamers in search of the site they'd call Home.

If they left from Commencement Bay, the mist on that winter day would have hung low, mingling the fringes of its clouds with the smoke off the steamships and the stacks of the factories on shore. As they pulled away from wharves, warehouses, coal bunkers, and mills, they would have seen a city rising on the hill behind them. The stone and wooden buildings were densely packed, dark and damp in the wetness; through the haze, an occasional hand-painted sign, a cone spire, a steeple, a chimney with its leeward smear of smoke stood in relief against the roofs. From the T-bars topping tall, knotted poles, electric wires extended in a crazy web above the muddy streets. Down below, the tracks of carriage wheels left imprints, their paths often avoiding the deep mires in the middle of the road. Here and there, a horse might be tied to a rail below a storefront canopy. A street car could be glimpsed between the buildings, its passengers huddled against the cold. The men in the boat would have been glad to be leaving it all behind.

This rough-hewn frontier city, a city of strangers, where one in five people had lived for less than five years, represented much of what these three men were rejecting. In 1889, Rudyard Kipling had visited this town that would call itself the City of Destiny, and after inhaling the sweet odor of sawdust and listening to the real estate speculators, he commented that Tacoma was, "literally staggering under a boom of the boomiest."[1] For a brief moment, city leaders believed it could rival San Francisco and New York, but the Panic of 1893 had shown that the feverish growth could not continue forever.

The economic collapse, brought on by over-speculation in the railroad industry, reduced millionaires to paupers. In Tacoma, a town whose fortune derived directly from the Northern Pacific Railroad, the formerly well-heeled took on boarders in their mansions, worked as janitors in their own buildings, even put bullets in their heads to end the misery and disgrace. There had been twenty-one banks in the city at the beginning of the year, but after all of the bank runs, only seven remained. The workers and poor suffered as well. Across the nation, at the height of the depression, between two and three million people, 20 percent of the workforce, were without jobs. The idle and aimless gathered around fires on the outskirts of towns, sharing whatever food they could scrounge. Hundreds of such men massed just outside Tacoma and attempted to follow their leader, a bouncer and occasional prize fighter named Jumbo Cantwell, over the mountains in an attempt to join Coxey's Army, an ill-fated march on Washington, D.C., to demand federal relief.

As Tacoma and the strife and turmoil it represented receded from view, the three men could see on a bluff above the bay one last symbol of hubris: the magnificent edifice of the Tourist Hotel. After the Northern Pacific Railway went bankrupt, it abandoned its support for this hotel, intended to be one of the best on the West Coast. Its partner, the Tacoma Land Company, could only afford to build the walls and roof, so while the spires, towers, and gables on the exterior resembled a French chateau, the interior remained unfinished. By 1896, the windows were boarded up, and the structure was a husk of a building, used to store shingles and other goods.

The men traded off the work of rowing. Oliver Verity, just over forty years old at the time, gripped the oars firmly with hands thickened by carpentry work, and his wiry, muscular frame distilled an intense energy into the strokes. His unruly hair stood above a face with sharp features and a thin chin, and he peered beyond the gunwales with a glint in his eye that mixed the restlessness of a pioneer with that of a radical.

When George Allen took over, his hands might have seemed smaller and softer by comparison, but this school teacher had more than a few calluses from the hard labor of odd jobs. Also in his forties, Allen wore a moustache and parted his hair on the side, and he liked to talk. No one but the three men knew for sure what they discussed that day, but ten years later, Allen recounted what might have been the thrust of their conversations: "We had heard and read many isms and had tried some of them with varying success. We wished to give each ism a chance to prove its usefulness to humanity."[2]

When the brawny blacksmith, Frank Odell, began pulling, the oars were gripped in thick palms that knew the weight of iron and the heat of a furnace.

Oliver A. Verity

George H. Allen

Frank Odell

He had a stout face with a thick moustache, and perhaps while the other two spoke of ideas, this practically minded man watched the shore slowly roll past.

As they approached Point Defiance, the city and its buildings, smoking mills, and fiery smelters gradually disappeared, and the tall conifers that remained—Douglas firs and cedars—edged their way up to the shore. Thick, helter-skelter branches crowded together into a canopy blocking out the view and rising above the water on tall bluffs. As they rounded the point, the slate-colored water concentrated into a mile-wide passageway called the Tacoma Narrows. Here tidal currents roiled the surface, and if the three men timed their journey correctly, they rode a flood tide through the Narrows.

The shore on either side was logged in some places, cut as clear as men with axes and crosscut saws could. Loggers and settlers usually tried to blast the stumps out with dynamite, burning them into blackened, amputated sentinels amid the brambles, but where stumps and slash remained, the incessant rains had bleached the wood to the color of bone. Still, large stretches of land resembled "the impenetrable wilderness of lofty trees" that Peter Puget and his crew on the *Catham* had gazed upon a century before as they explored this inland sea with Vancouver.[3] The three men in their rowboat in 1896 could see the same hoary, fissured trunks that Puget and his men had seen in 1778. Cabins and homesteads in the clearings were still rare sights in the immense thickets of greenery.

✗✗✗

ALL THREE WERE FAMILY MEN, with wives and children waiting their return to Tacoma. All hailed from other places: Verity from the Midwest, Allen from Ontario, Odell from Colorado. They were refugees from the failed utopian experiment at Glennis and had only a twenty dollar gold piece between them, currency enough for a new beginning.

Glennis had shown them what they did not want. This socialist colony had a brief existence twenty-seven miles outside of Tacoma, in the Cascades foothills. It was inspired by what Oliver Verity called "the Bellamy plan."[4] In 1888, the writer and journalist Edward Bellamy published *Looking Backward, 2000-1887*, a novel about an upper-middle-class Bostonian named Julian West who, through an accident of hypnosis, falls asleep in the nineteenth century and awakes on the brink of the twenty-first century. He finds a world where war, crime, labor unrest, crushing poverty, and other problems of his day have been solved.

A certain Dr. Leete serves as his tour guide to the future. The government, Leete explains, has taken over all industry, and everyone, men and women alike, receives educations and then serves in an Industrial Army. The president is the commander-in-chief of this vast, highly managed enterprise. Workers earn the same amount in credit, received from the government, regardless of their work, and material comforts are provided for equally. This new arrangement has created a world so perfect that the moral guideposts that Western civilization has used for millennia now seem unnecessary: "The ten commandments became well-nigh obsolete in a world where there was no temptation to theft, no occasion to lie either for fear or favor, no room for envy where all were equal, and little provocation to violence where men were disarmed of power to injure one another."[5]

In its day, *Looking Backward* was highly influential among the growing upper-middle class, selling two hundred and ten thousand copies by December 1889 and sparking a movement known as Nationalism. By 1891, a hundred and sixty-five Nationalist Clubs, where members read and discussed Bellamy's work had formed in twenty-seven states and the District of Colombia.[6] Although there is no record that the founders of Glennis participated in these clubs, they drank deeply from this zeitgeist.

Oliver Verity and a man named William Reed together donated a quarter section (one hundred and sixty acres) of land to the Glennis Cooperation Industrial Company, which was established on May 5, 1894. In its first year, Glennis appeared to be achieving its goals: "to own and operate manufactories, to acquire land, to build houses for its employees; to insure the employees against want, or the fear of want; and to maintain harmonious social relations on the basis of cooperation."[7] Membership grew from eight to thirty adults, and land was cleared, gardens planted, houses and workspaces built. But in the second year, problems large and small began to rupture the community. "Spring came late at that elevation (about a thousand feet) and gardens started slowly. The chickens did not lay as well as expected," Sylvia Allen, George's wife, told her granddaughter many years later. Sylvia herself had to work from dawn to dusk in the fields, the community kitchen, and a cooperatively owned soap factory. "There were others who did not seem to work as hard but shared equally."[8]

Those who lived through the experiment remembered other problems. The members of Glennis tasted firsthand the tyranny hidden like a clot in the heart of Bellamy's socialist idea. Oliver Verity put it this way:

> The desire of the many at Glennis to make bylaws restricting others from doing things that in reality were private matters, causing so many meetings which were noisy and bred inharmony from the diversified views of what should be done, not only made us lose interest in meetings, but finally disgusted us at the wrangles and disputes over petty matters.[9]

George Allen agreed: "Too many restrictions, which hampered the members, certainly made each one of us ill at ease and at last drove them gradually from the colony until only seven remained out of nearly thirty members."[10]

As much as Glennis was stricken by laziness and excessive rulemaking, it was the unethical practices of one of its founders that led to its demise. The board of directors appointed William Reed (who had donated eighty acres of land) as the Superintendent for Agriculture. Reed began ordering the work crews to improve the stretch of land he had once owned, and after getting free help clearing and planting, he demanded his plot back, claiming he had been insane when he first deeded it to Glennis. Rather than incur the legal fees of a court battle, community leaders decided to cede the land. As disgruntled and disillusioned members fled, they demanded a refund of the fifty dollars they'd paid to join the experiment. After selling the extant land and paying out those who left Glennis, all that remained was the twenty dollar gold piece shared between Oliver Verity, George Allen, and Frank Odell, but it was enough to nurture dreams of a new experiment.[11]

The three families retreated to Tacoma, where the adults spent many a night hashing and rehashing what had happened at Glennis and how they might avoid such mistakes in the future. The ideal of utopia, the possibility of organizing society along different lines, still burned within them. In many ways they embodied the spirit of their age. The late nineteenth century was rife with various progressive political philosophies that attempted to rearrange, reform, and revolutionize human society. In the Puget Sound region, utopian experiments sprouted like mushrooms upon the back waterways: Burley on a lagoon on the Kitsap Peninsula, Equality on Skagit Bay up north, Freeland on Whidbey Island, the Puget Sound Cooperative out on the Olympic Peninsula. Their founders were drawn to cheap, available land requiring only cross cut saw, muscle, and the will to clear it. Each of these experiments had their own distinct ideology, but nearly all of them were based on a socialist model where labor, commodities, and goods were shared collectively.

Nineteenth-century philosophies can often resemble manic, fever dreams that desperately and impossibly try to yank greedy, lazy humanity into an ideal state. Yet the nineteenth century was a manic, feverish time that was yanking humanity into the modern world. The United States was convulsing with unprecedented social, economic, and technological change. Factories, mills, production lines, railroads, turbines, dynamos, telegraphs, telephones, typewriters, elevators, skyscrapers, cameras, phonographs, motion pictures— these and many other innovations changed how people worked, lived, and conceived of themselves. And society itself was organizing in new, unexpected ways, with the bounty consolidated among a few magnates while the majority of workers were left with scraps. In 1890, the wealthiest 1 percent of families owned 51 percent of real and personal property, while the bottom 44 percent owned only 1.2 percent.[12] As this strange, new world emerged, it's not surprising that some people would attempt to implement their alternative vision of a brave, new world.

Around the table in Tacoma, many ideas were proposed, debated, and eliminated, and the founders of Home ended up with a model for a new community that seemed the exact opposite of Glennis. "After many discussions upon principles, and discarding of many of them, we agreed upon the necessity of retaining those that upheld the freedom of the individual from any or all coercive laws or methods, under conditions that made the possession of a home safe," remembered Verity. The members would follow two essential principles: "First, the personal liberty to follow their own line of action, no matter how much it may differ from the custom of the past or present, without censure or ostracism from their neighbors; second the placing of every individual on his or her own merits, thereby making them independent."[13] This new community would exist with as little organization as possible. There would be no leaders and no laws. Land would be owned collectively, but each member would be responsible for his or her own share. Participation in all work would be voluntary and rely on members' good will. The ultimate goal: a small patch of earth in the United States where happiness would thrive and prevail, a place that perhaps could even serve as a model for others to follow. Only later would they see, after other people pointed it out, that they had stumbled on an anarchist model for their colony.

The three men carried this shared understanding as they journeyed south into Puget Sound. None of them later said whether they had a specific destination or were scouting several possible sites. The most direct route to where they ended up would have taken them around the sandy bluffs on the southern tip of the Gig Peninsula into Hale Passage. In this stretch of salt water lying between Point Fosdick and Fox Island, the men would have found the rowing smooth and easy compared to the tumultuous Narrows. Then, as the waterway opened up to Carr Inlet, which arcs between Gig Peninsula to the east and Key Peninsula to the west, they would have approached a barely visible indentation in the expanse of land.

〤〤〤

I SLOW THE CAR AS WE PASS through pockets of fog along the Key Peninsula Highway. Tacoma is twenty-five minutes behind us, and the unfamiliar road twists and curves over the lumpy land, tunneling through the conifers. These tall trees cast disorienting spells instead of shadows. One moment, I catch a glimpse of water between the trunks—smooth and placid on this winter day—and in another, a patch of dense mist draws everything in close. I can barely see the rise and fall of the pavement. On either side of the road, only the occasional mailbox and the entrance to a driveway covered in pine needles and moss are visible. Don't ask me which direction is my own home because I no longer know, but I do know that Home is somewhere farther down this road.

I talked my wife into taking this Sunday drive because I've never been to Home. We crossed the Narrows Bridge, followed Highway Sixteen to Purdy, and then drove across the spit, passing a huge mound of oyster shells just beside the bay. At the end of the long narrow sand bar, the land sharply scooped the road upward and after a few curves, began loosely unspooling down the peninsula. Each succeeding fog patch has dissolved my faith that where I'm going is somehow connected to where I've been. Our house in Tacoma no longer seems just a short drive behind us.

Emily has not been feeling well lately, troubled by a heavy fatigue and vaguely upset stomach, so we don't talk much as we drive. I try to pay attention to my surroundings, but because this is my first time here, I don't absorb much. On the right side of the road, we approach a piece of equipment that looks like it was used to haul logs, an arch with two wheels on either side, its yellow paint grimed over with disuse. Then comes a little brown sign that reads "Welcome to Home" and a quick succession of small buildings and businesses. I notice in particular the vintage yellow and brown sign for Home Grocery and Feed, then the newer-looking fire station, and the wooden frame of a diner called Lulu's Homeport Restaurant and Lounge.

We turn at the blinking light and drive along the bay, the houses situated on the slope above us, a hodgepodge of buildings from various eras. It looks like any other waterfront community on Puget Sound. We go to the end of the drive, turn around and park near the boat launch beside the bare canes of the blackberry bushes.

The three men who founded Home would have seen only trees when they gazed upon this spot over a century ago from the water. As they pulled the oars through the water, they found a narrow bay with a brook flowing into its head and wooded hills rising on either side. At high tide, the calm, blue-green water sometimes resembled a pond in its stillness, but strong wind could bring slate-colored chop dappled with white foam. Low tide revealed a muddy, flat bottom, bountiful with shellfish. Except for a small clearing on the south side of the bay, Douglas fir and cedar trees covered the land. As they assessed the slope from the water, the founders of Home envisioned the trees gone and an anarchist utopia in its place.

)O)O)(

IN THE SUMMER OF 1896, Sylvia Allen held her fourth daughter, named Glennis for the place she was born, wrapped tightly in a blanket against the cool breeze. The engine thrummed through her body as she and her family rode the steamer to Home for the first time. Gazing toward the stern of the *Typhoon*, she could see the dissipating trail of wood smoke following the vessel and its wake rolling across the waters of Commencement Bay. The Allens had remained in Tacoma through the winter and spring so that George could continue to draw his teacher's salary and keep up the payments on the land, but now they were finally following the Odells and Veritys.

Through tall windows, she watched Tacoma's wharfs recede into the fog of the factories and mills. The benches inside were polished from the passengers who had ridden this steamship first in Portland, then in Grays Harbor, and now on the Tacoma–Henderson Bay route. Inside the long passenger cabin, the family's belongings were stacked in trunks that also vibrated to the motor. The smoke of the city eventually gave way to the wooded bluffs of Point Defiance. Here the ship turned, the propeller churning the emerald water as it angled for its run through the Tacoma Narrows.

As her three other daughters explored the boat for the first time, perhaps pressing against the guardrail on the rear deck to watch the tiny whirlpools following the ship, what was left unsaid between Sylvia and her husband George? While baby Glennis cooed and wriggled in her arms, what was expressed in glances? Photographs of Sylvia show her as an unsmiling woman. It was the style at the time to sit expressionless, or even frown, in portraits, but she doesn't look like a woman who smiled easily. In her younger years, she had brown hair, a round face, and a slender build, but as she raised her four daughters, her hair peppered with gray and her frame became more solid. Eventually, she would resemble a hard-working pioneer woman.

Unlike many women of her generation, she had graduated from college—she was the first woman to graduate with a four-year degree from the University of Toronto. While in school, she was introduced to many of the radical ideas circulating among the educated set. "My personal emancipation during my college years consisted of abandoning my corsets and refusing to wear rings in my pierced ears," she would later say.[14] She also met George, a regular at socialist, anarchist, and atheistic seminars, who by then was showing his restless nature. He had studied medicine, dentistry, horticulture, music, and literature, but decided to become a school teacher. After they married in 1884, she also taught for a while in Windsor, Ontario, but stayed home after she became pregnant with their first child. When their more traditional relatives kept pestering the couple about their absence from church services, they decided to move west to Tacoma, where George's father Oliver already lived. Then Sylvia dutifully, and perhaps reluctantly, accompanied her husband first to Glennis, and now to another experiment.

As much as she embraced radical ideas, Sylvia seems to have been a traditional mother and school teacher. "She was a strict disciplinarian," wrote her granddaughter. "It was said of her that when teaching she merely had to look at a naughty boy in the back row and he would 'straighten up' immediately. I remember gentle, loving smiles from this taciturn woman but never laughter."[15] She probably didn't smile much as she patted little Glennis, riding the steamer south through the roiling Narrows. This was the family's third big move since leaving the fertile flatlands of Ontario, and it is perhaps no coincidence that the founders called their new settlement Home. The only account that explains why they chose this name comes from Sylvia's granddaughter: "They were weary of moving."[16]

Home did not yet have a wharf, or even a float, so Captain Ed Lorenz dropped the family off in Lakebay, five miles south of their destination. Albert Sorenson, a young man who lived on the peninsula, met them at the landing and loaded their belongings onto his wagon. A thick forest rose on either side of the wagon trail, at times blocking out the sun, as the team of horses clomped toward Home. The Odells and Veritys were waiting for them, a lunch spread upon the porch of a single-story cedar-shake house, the first, and at that time the only, house built in Home. The three families gathered in the shade and ate. Still holding her daughter, what did Sylvia see in the tangles of ferns and brush clustered at the feet of massive tree trunks? While the men talked of Home City forming on the shores of Joe's Bay, could she help but see that they were closer to nothing than something?[17]

)()()(

Home's early years are not as well documented as later years. This was a time to drip sweat rather than spill ink. Until houses were built, each family lived for a while in huts slapped together from rough-cut lumber bought on credit. Over the summer, they lifted beams against the sky, building a second house, "The Welcome Cottage," for the Odells. Then, for the Allens, they got to work on a large, two-story house with a porch and cedar shingles for siding. They cleared land, chopped down trees, and blasted the stubborn stumps. They repaid Ed Lorenz, captain of the *Typhoon*, for passage to Home in cordwood for his steamer. "Many a weary head lay down at night to rest for the task of the morrow," recalled George Allen.[18]

Each family took two acres apiece along the shore of Joe's Bay and agreed that any other person joining the colony would also get two acres. Using statistics from a government agricultural report, they took the total acres of cultivated land in the United States, divided it by the entire population, and found the resulting number to be one and three-quarters acres per person. Based on their past experiences, they believed a family only needed an acre of carefully cultivated land to subsist; thus, two would provide bounty. Each family began raising poultry and vegetables on their two acres. Unlike the Glennis socialist experiment, each family would be responsible for improving their own land. In spite of this individualistic approach, the families cooperated much as other pioneers did. They knew that certain things, like raising a house, couldn't get done without a collective effort.

As their lives and the community began to take shape, they had more energy at night to discuss ideas. Of utmost importance was getting like-minded people to join them, and by 1897 Oliver Verity began publishing *New Era*. "WANTED," it announced in its first issue, "printers, gardeners, shoemakers, and practical men and women in all the different trades, to unite their labor and capital in establishing industries that will retain for the workers the products of their labor."[19] By reading this paper, or by word of mouth among radical circles, people were attracted to the community, coming from near and far to live on Joe's Bay. Billy King, farmer and teamster, traveled from Iowa with his wife, a skilled cook. White-bearded Hugh Thompson, a ship carpenter and Army veteran, brought his wife and family. Charles Penhallow, poet and hat varnisher by trade, journeyed with his wife Mattie from New England. Elum Miles arrived from Connecticut, and this elderly, scholarly-looking former Unitarian minister seemed out of place clearing land in a hickory shirt, grubby overalls, and lumberjack brogans.[20]

By early 1898 the community had grown to twenty-three people. The founders had originally resisted codifying their plan, but as more people joined, they began to see the value in having the barest of formal organization and sought incorporation into Pierce County. With the help of a Tacoma lawyer they drafted the articles of the Mutual Home Association, which would serve as a landholding body for the community. This document stated the goal of the association: "To assist its members in obtaining and building homes for themselves, and to aid in establishing better social and moral conditions." Anyone could join by paying into the treasury the cost of the land plus one dollar. Any improvements, such as buildings or gardens, would be the owner's personal property. "A certificate of membership shall be used only for the purpose of purchasing land," it further explained. "The real estate of this association shall never be sold, mortgaged or disposed of. A unanimous vote of all members of this association shall be required to change these articles of incorporation."[21]

The original seventeen subscribers elected the first officers of the association. Elum Miles became the president, Oliver Verity the secretary, and George Allen, Hugh Thompson, and H. B. Wren the trustees. These men would serve a year in these positions, with new officers elected at the annual meeting in January. The body wouldn't so much govern as see to the day-to-day operations of the association.

With growth and incorporation also came publicity. In February 1898, just a month after the community adopted the articles of the Mutual Home Association, a Tacoma journalist paid a visit. The unnamed writer of the article titled "Washington Colony of Anarchists" spent a few days in Home. "That they advocate the absolute abolition of the marriage tie, and perfect freedom and equality of the sexes, does not seem startling when you hear their views on other subjects," he commented.

> The wildest liberty, what would seem to "unadvanced" people unbridled license, is openly advocated, and these devoted adherents of anarchy claim that no evil can follow, or at worst not nearly so much as under "governmental" conditions. All restraint, they say, is and must be injurious. If there were no laws, we should not be able to break them. Thus crime would die of inanition and the perfect state ensue.

Speaking to his generally conservative audience in Tacoma, the newspaperman continued: "One would naturally conclude, on reading what has gone before, that these anarchists on Joe's Bay are dangerous citizens and their presence inimical to interests of the commonwealth." But then, somewhat surprisingly, he defended the community, saying that he was willing to raise his right hand and solemnly aver:

First, that among these women declaring such abominable heresies there is not one who is not now, and has not always been, an exemplary wife and mother, and that the imputation of unchastity would be an unwarranted complement to their personal charm. Second, that the men are in action the most fraternal of human kind, and while advocating and condoning the most abhorrent deeds, they are constantly occupied in acts of thoughtful kindness to each other and the outside world. Society stands in no danger from them, saving that of being talked to death.[22]

Given the venom and animosity the Tacoma press would later express toward the nest of anarchy just a short boat ride away, this first article seems like a strangely warm welcome.

✕✕✕

IT WAS SIGNIFICANT, and somewhat dangerous, that the colonists in Home identified themselves as anarchists. This prodigious sentence begins the entry on anarchism in the eleventh edition (1910-11) of the *Encyclopædia Britannica*:

> Anarchism, the name given to a principle or theory of life and conduct under which society is conceived without government—harmony in such a society being obtained, not by submission to law, or by obedience to any authority, but by free agreements concluded between the various groups, territorial and professional, freely constituted for the sake of production and consumption, as also for the satisfaction of the infinite variety of needs as aspirations of a civilized being.[23]

Originally written in 1905 by Prince Peter Kropotkin, one of the leading anarchist philosophers, this is a contemporary general definition of anarchism that the founders of Home would have agreed with. In the neutral tone of the encyclopedia entry, Kropotkin envisions how society might develop along anarchist lines, with people organizing themselves into mutually beneficial groups and existing without government to hinder progress.

> The voluntary associations which already now begin to cover all the fields of human activity would take a still greater extension so as to substitute themselves for the state in all its functions. They would represent an interwoven network composed of an infinite variety of groups

and federations of all sizes and degrees, local, regional, national and international—temporary or more or less permanent—for all purposes: production, consumption, and exchange of, communications, sanitary arrangements, education, mutual protection, defense of the territory, and so on.[24]

Anarchism, as presented here, is an optimistic philosophy with faith in the inherent moral strength of humankind. If humanity is stunted and flawed at present, the unnatural entity known as the state and its laws are to blame; throughout history, government has always been "the instrument of establishing monopolies in favor of the ruling minorities."[25] Anarchists do not see anarchy as a lawless bedlam of violence, something akin to Thomas Hobbes's "state of nature," where no government serves as an arbiter between those in conflict. No, anarchists see anarchy as harmonious cooperation among equals, with no government to enable the consolidation of wealth and power to a select few.

Yet most people of the era took a much different view of anarchism. Many considered it a pernicious philosophy that sought to rend the very fabric of the social contract. A more typical nineteenth-century view is reflected in definitions found in the *American Encyclopaedic Dictionary*, published in 1895. "Anarchy" is defined as "absence of government, and consequent disorder, as when 'there was no king in Israel, but every man did what was right in his own eyes.'" And an "anarchist" is simply someone who seeks to produce anarchy. Tellingly, the explanatory references quote from publications that were entered into the record during the Haymarket trial. "One man armed with a dynamite bomb is equal to one regiment of militia, when it is used at the right time and place. Anarchists are of the opinion that the bayonet and the Gatling gun will cut but a sorry figure in the social revolution," reads one blurb from an anarchist newspaper. Another declares: "Before you lies this blissful Eden. The road to it leads over the smoking ruin of the old world. Your passport to it is that banner which calls to you in flaming letters the word 'Anarchy.'"[26]

In America, the episode known as the Haymarket Affair solidified the popular image of anarchists as agents of night and chaos, plotting to usher in the noise and confusion of endless revolution. The May 15, 1886, issue of *Harper's Weekly* carried a two-page drawing that recreated, with some liberties taken in regard to the facts, an event that had happened ten days earlier in Chicago's Haymarket Square. It depicts the moment a bomb exploded among ranks of police officers who had just arrived to break up a gathering of anarchists and labor activists. Just to the right of center, a luminescent blast silhouettes a writhing police officer. To the left, on an oxcart, an anarchist with white locks and beard stands in a long coat, hand raised in a fist, mouth open with a shout. Whatever he's saying doesn't matter; he is clearly inciting violence against the policemen, the symbols of law and order. Just below, a dark-clothed man in a bowler hat fires a pistol into a cluster of policemen in double-breasted jackets, stars prominent on their chests. The guns of the policemen fire in all directions into the unruly mob around them.

This picture compressed into a moment the danger anarchism represented, ignoring the complicated forces at work behind this scene and distorting what had actually happened in Haymarket Square. The speakers had called for a nonviolent protest against the killings of workers who were striking for an eight-hour workday. Many in Chicago feared the gathering would turn into an insurrection of some kind, so the mayor wandered through the crowd, but he had concluded the demonstration was peaceful and left. The police, massed at a station nearby, grew uneasy as the hours passed, and they eventually decided to storm the square and order the crowd to disperse. The speaker on the oxcart, Samuel Fielden, was stepping down when someone threw the bomb. No one knew whose hand had lobbed it into the group of police. Yet this image and the media coverage that followed were powerful enough to fuel a hysterical fear of anarchists and contribute to a swift abortion of justice. Eight prominent Chicago labor leaders who identified themselves as anarchists were arrested and tried for the crime. Even though no evidence

Harper's Weekly
Depiction of "The
Anarchist Riot..."

of a direct connection between them and the bombing could be found, four of them died at the gallows, not for what they did but for what they believed. Among anarchists, these men became known as the Haymarket Martyrs, and their memory served as a reminder of the dangerous collusion of industry, government, and mass media.[27]

A string of bombings, assassinations, attempted assassinations, and other acts of violence rippled across Europe and the United States in the 1890s, also stoking fear of anarchism. In the preceding decades, certain European anarchist circles had begun to speak of "propaganda by the deed" as a viable method for bringing about revolution. The deed was a violent act that would spark revolution. "Permanent revolt in speech, writing, by the dagger and the gun, and by dynamite," wrote Kropotkin, who was initially among those who advocated this new approach, even if he never acted upon it himself. "Anything suits us that is alien to legality."[28] The assassination of political and economic leaders became known by the French word *attentat,* and it was supposed to awaken the proletariat and precipitate the unrest that would ultimately bring about an anarchist society. This idea captured the imagination of certain angry, disaffected young men in the late nineteenth century. In Spain and France, opera houses, cafés, and city streets shook with explosions, and when the guilty were caught, they often went to their deaths shouting "*Vive l'anarchie*!" In 1894, President Carnot of France was assassinated. In 1897 came the murder of Premier Canovas of Spain.[29] Never did these assassinations achieve revolution—almost always they led to the further repression of anarchism.

Even if these distant events had not been on the mind of readers of the 1898 article about the anarchists of Home, some would have remembered the attempted assassination of Henry Clay Frick in Pittsburgh six years before. The Homestead Strike of 1892 pitted the Carnegie Steel Plant against union steel workers. Andrew Carnegie had retreated to Europe, leaving his manager, Henry Clay Frick, to break the strike. As workers began to clash with hired Pinkerton detectives and sentiment began to rise against Frick, Alexander Berkman, a young and passionate Russian anarchist, saw his opportunity to carry out an *attentat*. "Society is a patient; sick constitutionally and functionally. Surgical treatment is often imperative. The removal of a tyrant is not merely justifiable; it is the highest duty of a revolutionist," Berkman later wrote in his memoir of the event. "To remove a tyrant is an act of liberation, the giving of life to an oppressed people."[30] Frick was the cancer needing removal, but Berkman's attempt was neither surgical nor successful. Claiming he was an employment agent, Berkman entered Frick's office, pulled a revolver and fired but only succeeded in wounding the man. Berkman spent sixteen years in jail, and Frick and his allies eventually used the failed assassination to more forcefully stamp out the strike.

As a result of these violent acts, the popular image of anarchists in the Gilded Age tended to ignore the differing interpretations of this political philosophy and lumped together people who may not have even agreed with each other. By the late 1890s, American anarchists were split into two factions. Anarcho-communists like Berkman were in one camp, believing that all property should be shared and that revolution should be carried out through propaganda by the deed. On the other side were individualist anarchists who believed that personal liberty was paramount, and that freedom should not be restricted by law or government authority; this group tended to advocate nonviolent resistance. A spectrum of philosophies existed among the founders of Home: while they seemed to embody the individualist approach, they aligned themselves in their later publications with anarcho-communists, perhaps because they could point to the fact that their land was owned in common. But if the growing community of anarchists on Joe's Bay practiced propaganda by the deed, the deeds were chopping down trees, raising roofs, planting gardens and orchards—all the work of building Home. When they did buy dynamite, it was for blasting stubborn tree stumps out of the ground.

✕✕✕

A copy of New Era lay on a countertop of Barbary Coast saloon, likely stained with spilled ale and soiled from the various hands it had passed through. Charles Govan picked it up and began reading in the dim light. Even with a few drinks in him, he was reading between the lines. The typography left something to be desired: the four-page broadside had three columns and was clearly the work of amateurs, but the stilted, awkward prose spoke of a group of people on the wooded shores of Puget Sound attempting to organize a community around anarchist principles. The words *liberty* and *happiness* were repeated again and again. For all of their good intentions, this little community obviously needed a professional printer like himself, and perhaps living in this tiny isolated town would help him clean up his life.

"A small, slender man, middle-aged, his hair commencing to gray, looking, as some said, like a Catholic priest of French stock from New Orleans, which, in fact, was his native city," was how one contemporary writer described Govan. "This man who, from his own open confession, had spent most of his years in dissipation, seems curiously to have received a stimulus to a more sober life from the anarchistic philosophy, which he had adopted as a relief to the soul in its remorse, much indeed as a priest would have taken religion."[31] Govan traveled north and rode the steamer to Home, but by the time he walked down the gangplank onto the float in Joe's Bay, *New Era* was defunct.

Govan found eager partners in reviving the newspaper in Home. He acquired an Army press and set up shop in a shed-like building made of slat boards that stood on end. Founders Allen and Verity, along with colonists Miles and Penhallow, helped put together the paper. The first issue appeared on Wednesday, May 11, 1898, bearing the title *Discontent* in a serif font that added embellished curlicues to the *C* and the *O*. Just below, in type so small that a reader would have to bring the paper close to read it, was the phrase *The Mother of Progress*. Nowhere does the paper mention the source of the title, but perhaps the learned, white-bearded Elum Miles had read Charles Dudley Warner's 1874 essay that states: "For, as skepticism is in one sense the handmaid of truth, discontent is the mother of progress. The man is comparatively of little use in the world who is contented."[32] Or perhaps this connection between discontent and progress had simply entered the vernacular of radicals and reformers of the day.

Whatever the origins of the title, the paper boldly declared that it would "battle for the freedom of the human race from tyranny and superstition of all kinds and sorts." The editors aligned themselves with anarcho-communism but also articulated their particular brand of anarchism: "Anarchy demands absolute individual sovereignty, the right of the humblest individual to hold and express his opinions, to live his own life and mind his own business; that no one shall assume to rule over any other or to attempt to compel others to conform to his ideas of what constitutes the best means of securing the general welfare." But they did not wish to even impose anarchism on everyone: "A tyrant calling himself an Anarchist is as much a tyrant as any other." [33] Their columns were open to liberal views of all kinds, but they especially invited anarchist writers. The only restrictions placed on contributions were space and literary merit.

Discontent was never seen simply as Home's newspaper, but as a publication that would interest anarchists and free thinkers across the country. The contributors of the articles, tracts, criticisms, and other pieces lived in all corners of the U.S. In the first issue, for example, William Smith from Boston wrote an article titled "Is 'Sin' Forgivable?" Reprints from other radical journals were also published, often on a range of topics of interest to free thinkers. The second issue contained a piece called "Fashion Among Free Lovers" by E. C. Walker, first published in the East Coast anarchist newspaper *Lucifer.*

A regular column variously titled "Ideas and Criticisms," "War Talk," "Potpourri," and "Mélange" came from F. A. Cowell in San Francisco. A typical column leaped from topic to topic across triangles of asterisks: an account of Emma Goldman's local speaking engagement; the story of a man stealing to feed his family and then sentenced to ten days in jail; a recap of a heated debate at an anarchist meeting about whether anarchism applies to natural laws; a mention of the czar of Russia giving the prince of Montenegro an Easter gift of thirty thousand repeating rifles. "No more appropriate season than Easter could have been selected for such a present. It so pointedly shows the hypocrisy of Christianity," Cowell commented.[34] Whatever the topic, the tone remained consistently sarcastic.

✕✕✕

EVEN THOUGH *DISCONTENT* SOUGHT a national audience, its pages also served as a venue for the writings of the residents of Home. In this way, it began to express the spirit of the community taking shape on the shores of Joe's Bay. In a regular column titled "Problem Solved," the president of the Mutual Home Association, Elum Miles, analyzed the economic, banking, and monetary system, "a system that has for ages enriched and barbarized the few, ruined and debased the masses; that has blighted the hopes of millions of earth's noblest sons and daughters and swept great nations into heaps of ruins."[35] Charles Penhallow contributed poems, one of which sang the reasons for his attraction to Joe's Bay:

> I there a promise feel,
> That in a future great
> I'll find a realm that's truly free
> From taint of church or state.

Where each will live for all:
Where all will care for each;
And in an atmosphere of love,
They'll practice what they preach.[36]

Penhallow's verse struck a theme—practicing what they preach—that appeared again and again in the writings of the residents of Home. *Discontent* was their place to preach, and Home was their place for practice.

Liberty and happiness were the watchwords of Home's philosophy. Individual freedom was of utmost importance, as long as one's behavior did not impinge on others. "The foundation of all associations should be absolute liberty; the liberty of each to assert his or her own individuality. The greatest progress can only be made by the unfolding of each and every mind to its fullest capacity. All restrictive measures must of necessity retard the evolution of humanity," wrote Oliver Verity. "The establishing of the Mutual Home Association opens up a way to many of obtaining a home. Looking to this end, we invite the co-operation of all those who believe in throwing off the oppressive yoke of God, Government, and Grundy to unite their efforts with ours to establish a condition or community where we can assert true manhood and womanhood."[37]

They considered themselves an example to others throughout the world, a kind of anarchist City upon the Hill, but in "Freedom, the Natural Remedy," George Allen doubted that applying anarchist principles across the country would work, at least at first:

Would the human race be happy immediately on all the barriers being struck down? No; because this iniquitous system has produced a lot of distorted animals in human form that several years, or even decades, might be needed to get man into the full effect of perfect freedom. But do you think that this is a good reason why we should not try the only right remedy—freedom? Any person who knows half the terrible consequent evils produced by governmental system will see even in this transitory period that things could not be made much worse.[38]

Although these men weren't proposing original ideas, these passages reflect the kinds of words heard in the meeting rooms and vegetable gardens, on the footpaths and the single dirt road stretching along the shore, and in the shade of the fir and cedar trees up the hill. Liberty and happiness—these words saturated the atmosphere of Home, and in the small office, the editors of *Discontent* transmuted them into ink upon paper so that they might rain down upon the rest of the country and provide nourishment.

The regular column "Association Notes" reported on day-to-day life in the colony. In the summer months, they ventured in search of blackberries: "A ramble through the wild wood in search of them is highly appreciated by both old and young, even though the pails are not filled to overflowing." During the salmon run, they trolled the bay, "landing fine specimens of the finny tribe."[39] The column mentioned the arrivals and departures of residents and various visitors, such as Mrs. Scannel and her three children from Tacoma, the first of summer vacationers, who came to enjoy the pure country air and "study Anarchy in practice."[40] Comrades Swigart, Smith, and La Franz dropped in from Equality Colony, the socialist utopian experiment up the Sound. A barber with the surname Herman from Philadelphia "swings an ax and handles a crosscut saw as though he expected to clear everything in sight. As soon as the blisters on his hands heal up, he thinks he will be a co-operator among us."[41]

Contributors to *Discontent* wrote too of recreational and educational activities, such as the mental science class that met, for a while, every Sunday afternoon at two o'clock. "The mental science theory appears to give a logical answer to many perplexing questions that have in the past seemed unanswerable."[42] That fall of 1898, people became more interested in singing lessons: "A singing school was organized last Sunday with nearly all the residents of our community in attendance and G. H. Allen as instructor. This feature promises to be not only instructive but very pleasant. It will meet every Sunday at 2 p.m. in the schoolhouse."[43] *Discontent* noted the progress of work, as well. In July, residents bought a steam-powered drag saw for $457, with $174 down and the rest due in installments. They estimated that it would put up to twenty men to work, but several months passed before it was running properly.[44] By October, *Discontent* announced: "The engine as a grubber is a daisy. The cost of clearing an acre of ground will undoubtedly be greatly lessened. The boys are making for tall timber with it."[45]

ⅩⅩⅩ

WHEN MARTIN DADISMAN and his son Harry arrived in October of 1898, there were no more than a dozen houses dotting the shoreline of Joe's

Bay. The colonists could count a number of significant signs of progress. A regular school had been established, with Sylvia Allen teaching a dozen or so children. At the head of the bay, pilings had been driven into gray silt for a new bridge, and waiting for the planks of a walkway, pilings also stood in parallel lines from the shore to the float where the steamer docked. Several men had cut a tram road into the woods to speed the journey of the logs to the bay. Two hundred cords of wood lined the shore, ready for shipment. But the community, with its unpainted pioneer homes of graying lumber, fences of slanting cedar slats, and dirt paths between the brambles and charred stumps, was barely an imprint in the wilderness. At the time, between forty and fifty people lived in Home, but the moss and the vines, the blackberry and salal could have easily spread back down the slope and erased the two years of work to build Home.

But Dadisman saw something that he liked. Born into a wealthy family in Virginia, he was attracted to unconventional, radical views. "His ideas are in general use today, but in those times, they were almost unheard of," remembered his son David. "On our farm in Virginia dad had a black man working for him, and he sat at the table with us. The neighbors found out and threatened to tar and feather dad and ride him out on the rails. He was so aggravated by their attitude that he decided he was going to get out of there."[46] As he wandered the country, he drifted west and stayed for a time in Equality Colony on Skagit Bay, but he disliked that the work wasn't shared equally there: a few industrious people did everything while others loafed about. Dadisman appreciated that in Home if a person was going to make it, he had to do it by his own initiative.

Then in his forties, Dadisman had a receding hairline that highlighted his prominent brow. A long, patrician nose angled down his face, pointing to a narrow, angular chin. His close-set, intelligent eyes easily aligned into a distant gaze. Since he was a man of means, his membership was a boon for the growing colony. He immediately began buying land adjacent to the settlement and deeding it to the Mutual Home Association. In November of 1898, he made sixty-four acres available for settlement. "This tract is especially advantageous for residences as it commands a fine view of the bay and surrounding country," reported *Discontent*.[47] Only months after he arrived in Home, the Association elected Dadisman treasurer.[48] In the following years, he would purchase an additional eighty acres and open this

The Verity family

land to colony settlement, so that when the Mutual Home Association had Home platted in 1901, there would be two hundred and seventeen acres in all.

✕✕✕

EMILY AND I GET OUT OF THE CAR to walk around on my first visit to Home. I notice immediately that nearly all of the houses are oriented toward the water. Most of the old historical photographs show the colonists standing outside their houses, gazing either at the camera or out of the frame. What I had not considered was that those who were looking away, probably had their eyes on the water, like Mrs. Verity, the woman wearing a patterned dress who is turned sideways in one photograph. Water surrounded and set apart the original Utopia described by Sir Thomas Moore. It seems appropriate then that water forms a natural feature of life in Home, but this fact raises a more practical consideration, as well: with such clear views of the bay, everyone could see and hear what was happening on the bay, almost as if it were happening in their own homes. Lately, I've been reading about the nude bathing episode that set in motion a conflict that would contribute to the dissolution of the colony. No wonder it had such a potent impact.

Today the water looks slate gray and cold, its smooth surface untouched by wind. I'm checking out a sailboat floating like a desolate and forgotten vessel, its stays and shrouds slack, its hull slick with algae, when Emily discovers the plaque just off from the road, hidden between the bushes. We stand in the damp shaggy grass sprinkled with brown leaves and read its synopsis of the history of Home, of its founding in 1896, of the establishment of the Mutual Home Association in 1897, and the addition of land by Martin Dadisman in 1898.

> A school, wharf, warehouse, and community hall were built by the industrious settlers. The residents were people of radical yet tolerant thought. *New Era, Discontent,* and *Agitator* were widely circulated Home publications that attracted growth. The content of the papers reflected the community's interest in government, free speech, women's rights and other issues of concern to society.

Just below, a second plaque affixed to the upright concrete slab lists members of the Mutual Home Association and other early pioneers. Some of the names already stand out from their mention in the histories of Home: James and Mary Adams, Martin and Mary Dadisman, Jay and Esther Fox, Philip Van Buskirk, Gertie Vose. Others listed there remain anonymous, leaving behind for me only the strange, conjuring sounds of their names: Bessie Brout, Henry and Fannie Hanson, Lucille Mint, H. B. and Hellen Wren.

Back in the car, we drive north and stop in Key Center at a drive thru espresso stand called the Close to Home Café. Emily orders a decaf cappuccino, I get an Americano, and as we sip our drinks on the way home, she comments on how good it is. Even though it's decaf, it cuts through the sluggishness she's felt all day.

Two weeks from now, she will leave a pregnancy test on a window sill for me to find, its two solid lines indicating why she had not felt well and showing us that another had been traveling with us that day.

XXXX

As 1898 came to a close, the weather remained mild. On December 29, colonists bragged in "Association Notes" of gardens still producing vegetables. Cabbage, cauliflower, and carrots were still flourishing in the rain, drawing nutrients from soil that had just a short time before sustained a forest. Snow had dusted the landscape and roofs, but it melted into slush by the afternoon.

A few days before the New Year, the children told their parents that there would be a Children's Jubilee on the Eve. The old folks were expected to do nothing but provide refreshments and enjoy themselves. When the adults gathered at the schoolhouse, they found it had been arranged into a theater, with rows of chairs facing a makeshift stage. The children performed a variety show. Together, all the boys and girls sang songs such as "Come All Jolly Sportsmen," "The Peddler's Son," and "Three Blind Mice." In between, children in pairs or by themselves recited short works like "The Screech Owl" and "Ring out Wild Bells."[49]

In the glow of oil lamps, the parents enjoyed hearing the children's voices and applauded their accomplishment. George and Sylvia Allen grinned at the sound of their daughters' voices. Resting briefly from logging and writing for *Discontent*, Oliver Verity beamed as his daughter Macie spoke in a dialogue. And the face of Frank Odell—the last founder of Home, who never shared his thoughts in Home's newspapers and who would soon leave the colony—shone with pride as his daughter Mabel read aloud. As the program drew to a close in the schoolhouse that night, did the three men look at one another? Did they remember how almost three years before they had built a boat and ventured in search of a place that they would call Home? If they did, they might have felt that their efforts were finally taking hold, that the roots of this community, just like those of fruit trees planted up the hill, were finally pushing deep into the duff and mud beside the bay.

After the program, the boys and girls served supper to the parents, and then they announced that everyone would play games. "This isn't going to be turned into a political meeting," one young girl indignantly remarked, probably remembering many nights when the parents were immersed in abstruse and boring talk.[50] The room filled with laughter, for the parents were willing to humor the children. The people of Home began playing cards, dominoes, checkers, or chess, waiting for the New Year to turn.

Far off over the Pacific Ocean, a weather pattern was developing that would funnel down between the Olympic and Cascade mountain ranges and bring snow. The fat snowflakes would begin sifting down out of the sky on January 5, burying the cabbage, cauliflower, and carrots in their beds, halting all work of hauling logs on the tram road, and reaching two feet in depth. The writer of "Association Notes" would have to admit the mistake of bragging about the balmy weather. Except for the shrieks of joy as children slid down the hill, the land around Joe's Bay would briefly return to the silence it had once known. But this would be in the future, in the New Year; for now, everyone was playing games, murmuring in the warmth, waiting for the minute hand to bring in the last year of the nineteenth century.

Life at Home: Shelter

JOE KOPELLE AND FRANZ ERKELENS lived in a tree house on the edge of Home. Nearby on the ground, they hosted many a meal in the canvas tent that served as a dining room. There was rarely a vacant spot at the dinner table but always a spare seat. They'd just saw off a section of log, adjusted for the visitor's height, thump it onto the boards, and roll it into place.

Joe Kopelle remembered the setting as if it were a vision of Big Rock Candy Mountain. The fare was bountiful and varied. Franz usually cooked, but a guest sometimes commandeered the stove: a vegetarian, Tildenite, Hungarian, or some other chef professing a superior diet. The person at the head of the table could lean slightly to dip a cup in the cool clear spring that ran beside the platform. The person to his or her right could reach everything on the stove without getting up, as well as the strong box kept as a cooler in the creek behind the platform.

The tree house even had an automatic dishwasher. Franz and Joe would slide the dishes, pots, and pans into the stream, and the current stripped away the remaining food. The trout would jab their heads inside the cast iron pots and nibble off any stubborn remnants. Once a boy was lying on his stomach, letting the water run through his fingers, and one of these fish swam into his fingers. "Look what I caught, mom!" he exclaimed, lifting the writhing creature out of the water.

"Hey, young fellow, put that dish-washer back in the creek!" Franz said with a laugh. "He's our friend!"[1]

Wearing a broad-brimmed hat and thick moustache, Joe had first gazed upon the tree when he was investigating the property. Long ago, strong winds had sheared off the top, leaving a massive trunk. In the years since the storm, new growth had sent shoots skyward that were stout enough to support a platform. Joe cut them level with the main trunk, nailed slats like a circular staircase up the trunk, and then constructed a floor. Four low walls and a roof provided shelter. Franz and Joe slept on bunk beds softened with cedar boughs and read books from a well-stocked shelf. "From up there the air was warm and a grand view could be had of the bay," recalled Joe. "We could see all that went on in every direction."[2]

Although Joe claimed he was drawn to the spot because he was a landscape gardener by trade and "a worshiper of nature's wonders," his decision to move to this particular parcel in 1908 also reflected that most of the prime lots in Home had been taken.[3] "The establishing of the Mutual Home Association opens up a way to many to obtaining a home," Oliver Verity had written; since he first published these words in *Discontent* in 1898,[4] a succession of people had answered his call.

A time-lapse film of the community's growth would show the Douglas firs on the hillside falling one after the other as men notch their trunks, whack with axes, then cut with crosscut saws, and roll the logs down toward the water. With the land cleared, acre by acre, the colony members converge to sink posts and piers into the loam for a foundation, raise the wall frames, and lift the roof beams. Soon enough walls are sheathed in board and batten or bevel siding, enclosing and protecting spaces that just a season ago knew only the shelter of trees and the course of wind through the forest. This happens over and over again as more and more members join the Mutual Home Association. Hammers drive nails, shovels dig wells, hands stretch stockade and slat fences between parcels. Roads and paths slice across the hillside, gardens and orchards are planted in neat rows, and in some places ornamental vines begin to climb toward the gables. As the hasty procession of the film progresses, the houses get larger and more impressive: there is the Allens' shingle-sided house with a sagging two-story porch and the Kings' huge box-style house with a wrap-around porch.[5] By the time Joe Kopelle arrives in 1908, around two hundred people live in Home in over fifty homes.[6]

"You'll find it damp," people told Joe when he bought the lot,[7] and perhaps this is why he built the tree house; or perhaps he thought it would be easier to live in the tree than remove it. In the accounts of his tree house, he only explained what he did, not why, but he certainly enjoyed his rustic living arrangement. Although Franz left in 1910, Joe stayed until 1917. Only then, when the shipyards were booming in Tacoma during the war, did he climb down through foliage that still grew upon the shoots and set foot upon the ground for good. He worked a while in the city, and when he returned to Home, he moved into a house. What he remembered of the cold seasons, of shivering through wet and windy nights, he kept to himself; when he spoke of his famous tree house, it was always summertime.

CHAPTER TWO

The Anarchists Must Go

THE DAY THAT NOBODY SHOT the President dawned like any other September day in Home. Milk cows lolled in the shade beneath the trees. Chickens pecked at the scratch inside their pens. As people walked along shore, following the route that only a month before had been widened into a road, a flock of ducks paddled deeper into Joe's Bay and lifted into flight.

The sunlight itself had ripened, the brilliance of late summer condensing and darkening with the chill that crept up from the water at night. In the waning glow, tomatoes weighed on the vines. "Ours are the pride of the Sound," residents bragged. "If you doubt it, come sample them."[1] But as always happens at this time of year, as if beckoned by the September light, the spiders had emerged too. Their webs could be found everywhere, stitching together house beams, window panes, fence posts, fronds of sword ferns, limbs of fruit trees, and even the bent vines of the tomato plants.

In September 1901, eighty-two residents lived upon the east-facing slope above Joe's Bay, and many were intimately familiar with the legal consequences of publishing matter considered obscene by their contemporaries. Seventy-five-year-old Lois Waisbrooker, now busy with writing and editing her monthly publication about women's rights and issues, could count herself among them. Tall and with angular features that one contemporary compared to Abraham Lincoln's, she had already written and published over a half-dozen books, including the novels *Helen Harlow's Vow* and *A Sex Revolution*. Her critiques of the institution of marriage and advocacy of free love had gotten her arrested in Topeka, Kansas, but she accepted this trouble as just another part of agitating against the Comstock laws and all the other federal and state statues that restricted free speech. "If prison will advance the work, I am ready," she wrote.[2] And so she was putting out *Clothed with the Sun*, a newspaper whose title might suggest that it advocated nudity but in fact was a reference to the Book of Revelation.

James Adams, who had lived in Home for several years, was basking in his recent opportunity to describe Home to the general populace. The *Tacoma Evening News* had published his letter explaining the philosophy at the heart of the colony:

We are neither Anarchists nor free lovers in the accepted definition of these terms by beef-necked moralists. As Anarchists, we believe that if nature's laws are diligently studied, and strictly observed, that is all that is necessary to insure man's salvation now, and for all time to come. As free lovers we believe that individualism means that we have the inalienable, constitutional, and individual right to love whom we may, to love as long or short a period as we can, to change that lover every day if we please; and with that neither God, devil, angel, man or woman has any right to interfere.[3]

This argument seemed a little odd coming from Adams, a white-bearded septuagenarian who had been happily married to his wife for almost fifty years, but like many in Home, he believed in and advocated the idea of absolute freedom.

After relocating from Boston to Home that summer, James Ferdinand Morton, Jr., had taken over as editor of *Discontent: the Mother of Progress*, the colony's newspaper. In his thirties, with a full head of wavy red hair, a moustache, and a broad chin, Morton had graduated from Harvard and was the grandson of the composer of the song "America." After rejecting his patrician upbringing, he converted to anarchism and became known as a lecturer who could hold forth on any number of burning issues. Nowadays, he primarily occupied himself with pulling together copy, keeping up with submissions, and writing his weekly column, "Off and On." The printer, James Govan, cranked out hundreds of papers each week, sending them to both coasts and even to Yokohama, Japan. In the newspaper office—a

The Office of
Discontent

structure that had been enlarged but still resembled a shed—a recently acquired mailing machine printed out the addresses, and a small, affable collection of neighbors gathered each week to wrap the papers and affix the labels. The papers then went to Mattie Penhallow, the postmistress of Home, and were bundled with the outgoing mail.

Perhaps these swollen mail bags stood on the shore as the daily steamer from Tacoma pulled into Joe's Bay, bearing news of the wounded president. In the days before radio and highways, the water surrounding the Key Peninsula formed a barrier across which everything but clouds and birds traveled at the speed of prow. As one of the local boys rowed the bags out to the float and greeted the ship, someone returning from Tacoma, one of the shipmen, or even Captain Ed Lorenz himself, could have told them that President McKinley had been shot, that he was wounded but still alive, that the assassin called himself an anarchist.

Outsiders would later claim that Home rejoiced. If anything, as word spread from house to house, the hillside was quiet that night as residents absorbed the stories in the *Evening News*. Although they certainly did not agree with McKinley's policies, many of them feared that the assassination would "inaugurate an era of persecution against all who are unsatisfied with existing conditions."[4]

XXX

ON THE OTHER SIDE OF THE COUNTRY, President McKinley had been standing on a raised dais in the Temple of Music, rotund and stolid as a boulder, greeting the throngs at the Pan-American Exposition in Buffalo, New York. A man who called himself Nobody waited in line, his right hand covered with a clean, white handkerchief. The Secret Service agents thought he was a nobody too, just another pale-faced worker in his Sunday best waiting to press his palm into the hand of the president of the United States. They were eyeing the tall, muscular black man standing behind him.

McKinley raised his hand toward the next in line. Nobody approached, his lifted hand still covered in a handkerchief, and squeezed the trigger of the .32-caliber pistol hidden just beneath. Twice he fired, hitting the president first in the chest and then the stomach. Before Nobody could fire another shot, Jim Parker, the black man just behind him, knocked the gun to the floor.

"Cries welled up from a thousand throats and a thousand men charged forward to lay hands upon the perpetrator of the crime," described one Tacoma newspaper.[5] For a few frantic moments, it seemed a thousand hands grabbed at Nobody's arms, chest, and legs, yanking him away from the president. A pair of hands even found Nobody's throat and began to squeeze. But Nobody was so determined to see what he'd done that he twisted out of the chokehold to look upon the bloodied president, slumped on the dais. This audacious gaze so enraged a Secret Service agent that he broke it with his fist.

They took him to the Buffalo police headquarters. A police blockade held back the crowd outside howling for a lynching. Nobody sat calmly on a cot inside his cell and spoke with a detective. He first gave his name as Fred Neiman, said his home was in Detroit, and that he had been in Buffalo for about a week. None of the officers talking to him knew German. His last name in German meant Nobody. "I am an Anarchist and I did my duty," Nobody said.[6]

⟫⟨⟫⟨

ON THE EVENING OF SEPTEMBER 6, 1901, crowds swirled around the bulletin boards outside the newspaper offices in Tacoma, wailing or cheering as bad or good news was posted. One face in the crowd belonged to a large, powerfully built Swedish fisherman. He stopped a passing man, looked down at him, and asked how many times the president had been shot.

"Twice, I think," the short man replied.

"I am sorry the first did not kill him," commented the fisherman.

The short man knew a traitor when he heard one, and he charged with such ferocity that the fisherman retreated across the street. "The small but patriotic American," as one newspaper called him, chased the object of his fury, and in front of the Oxford Saloon, he leapt upon the fisherman's broad back and bit his ear.

The fisherman groaned in pain, and trying to shake off his assailant, attracted the crowd's attention. Somehow everyone learned of the fisherman's treacherous words, and when he finally broke free of the small but patriotic American, a storm of fists and feet began to pummel him. He ran from the onslaught into the Oxford Saloon. The mob overturned chairs, tables, and whatever else was in its way as the now bruised and bloody fisherman scrambled for the back entrance. When they caught him at the Eleventh Street Bridge, they beat him until he could no longer stand. When their fury was spent, they jerked the man to his feet and spoke to his smeared and pulpy face, ordering him to cross the bridge. If he returned, they threatened death.

As the fisherman limped across the span, one man broke from the crowd and ran halfway toward him. Turning around, he yelled, "Boys, let's throw him from the bridge!"

"No, no, he's had enough," replied the mob in chorus. But when another man expressed sympathy for the fisherman, suggesting that they had perhaps treated him too harshly, fists squeezed his shirtfront and shook the doubter until he recanted.[7]

"There are times when laws seem to be suspended. This was such a time," commented *The Tacoma Daily Ledger* on its opinion page, condoning the rough handling of the Swedish fisherman and anyone else who made the mistake of voicing a contrary opinion. "The person capable of such an expression is getting more than he deserves when permitted to live in a free country. There is no form of punishment provided by statute."[8]

)O(O(

AS I SIT BEFORE A COMPUTER in the Microform Newspapers Collection of Suzzallo Library at the University of Washington, the pages of *Discontent* blur into a gray mass, punctuated by the black splotches of the title. I stop the machine to check the date, May 2, 1900; not even close. I want to see the issue published on September 18, 1901, when the residents of Home began to respond to McKinley's assassination. I requested this reel of microfilm through interlibrary loan, hoping that it will fill in the blanks of the incomplete reel I've been using; the issues jump from September 11, 1901, which has no mention of McKinley even though it was published four days after the shooting, to November 13, 1901. This two-month hole creates a maddening gap, an impassable washout just as the terrain gets interesting. One moment, I'm reading something that seems frozen in the amber of the languorous time before the assassination—James Adams's article praising the fertility of Puget Sound and cataloging the bounteous crops and orchards of Home's neighbors—and the next, *Discontent* and Adams himself are thick into the consequences of the assassination.

But what happened in Home in between? For now, the only sources I have are the Tacoma newspapers, with all their biases, and the writings of historian Charles LeWarne. Back in the 1960s, he was able to view a complete run of *Discontent* owned by a former resident of Home who is now deceased. LeWarne writes that the community responded with considerable apprehension and even includes a quote from Morton that predicts that the assassination would lead to persecution. But there are questions only the September 18 issue of *Discontent* can answer. Where on the page was the quote taken from? What else did Morton express in his verbose prose? Were there other responses? And what was happening in "Home News"? This section has become my favorite, giving random glimpses into the daily affairs of the colony. Who was coming and going from Home? What about the progress on Abner Pope's house or the slashing of Gertie Vose's two acres? How many pounds of tomatoes were harvested? It consoles me to know that ordinary life continues amidst the torrent of larger historic events.

On the computer screen, the pages trundle past describing July and August of 1901 in Home, then comes September, and the coverage drops off at the exact same place. September 18, then November 13. I roll back and forth just to make sure, beginning to feel as if I've been slowly and carefully unwrapping a mummy, only to find that the body disappeared long ago.

)⟨O⟩⟨O⟩⟨

NOBODY FINALLY GAVE HIS NAME: Leon Czolgosz. He admitted that he was from Cleveland, Ohio. The Tacoma newspapers published his confession on the front pages, in black borders:

> I never had much luck at anything and this preyed upon me. It made me morose and vicious but what started the craze to kill was a lecture I heard some time ago by Emma Goldman. She was in Cleveland, and I and other anarchists went to hear her. She set me on fire. Her doctrine that all rulers should be exterminated was what set me thinking so that my head nearly split with pain. Miss Goldman's words went through me, and when I left the lecture I made up my mind that I would have to do something heroic for the cause I loved.[9]

In interrogation after interrogation, Czolgosz insisted that he alone had planned and executed the diabolical act, but the newspapers and investigators could not reckon that this man, whose foreign name few could pronounce, had acted on his own initiative. Many officials held the firm conviction that he was but an actor in an anarchist plot. As a kind of proof of this conspiracy theory, the police rounded up known anarchists around the country, many with names that also challenged the American tongue: Abraham Isaak, Hippolyte Havel, Enrico Travaglio, Clemens Pfuetzner, Alfred Schneider. Secret Service detectives on the trail of the prime mover in the alleged plot, Emma Goldman, provided further validation.

Once in custody, the anarchists in Chicago admitted that they had met Czolgosz. The previous summer the young, clean-cut man had crashed several anarchist gatherings, awkwardly calling people he barely knew "comrade" and asking if he could attend "secret meetings." He told them that he had heard Goldman speak in Cleveland and traveled to Chicago to learn more, but his fervent, clueless intensity troubled the anarchists he met. The editor of the anarchist newspaper *Free Society*, Abraham Isaak, believed this strange loner was a government spy and published a warning about him just five days before the assassination: "His demeanor is of the usual sort, pretending to be greatly interested in the cause, asking for names, or soliciting aid for acts of contemplated violence."[10]

As the week after the shooting progressed, though, these kinds of subtle details did not register in the maelstrom of news coverage. Contrapuntal to headlines about the president's health were headlines about the hunt for Emma Goldman and the anarchist conspiracy. On September 10, the Queen of the Anarchists dominated the front page. The *Evening News* described her arrest in Chicago beneath the banner headline "What Would You Do with Emma?" Police had finally found her disguised as a Swedish woman named Lena Larson, in a Chicago home. Once the lawmen had her in custody, they gave her the third degree, knocking a tooth loose and shining bright lights into her eyes, trying to get her to admit to a conspiracy. But she remained defiant. "Am I accountable because some crack-brained person puts a wrong construction on my words?" Goldman asked her inquisitors. When she asserted that she never advocated violence, that she did not know the assassin, that he had acted alone, most thought her words were as good as lies. It was noted that she could pronounce Czolgosz's name with the greatest of ease.[11]

XOXOX

R*EGARDLESS OF WHETHER* there was a conspiracy, the opinion pages of Tacoma newspapers called anarchists *snakes, serpents, adders, vipers, mongrels, vermin*. And what had allowed this vile brood to infest the land? The very liberty granted each citizen by the Constitution of the United States. While McKinley lay convalescing from his wounds, some proposed extreme solutions. "Freedom of speech has run mad. It is without limitations. Any fool may blurt his treason and inspire murder without fear of punishment. The man who advocates the assassination of a president merits hanging from the same scaffold with the man who makes the attempt," declared the *Daily Ledger* in an op-ed titled "Exterminate the Anarchists."[12]

And on the Sunday after the shooting, priests and ministers in Tacoma pulpits joined the chorus, often echoing the very words of the newspapers. Reverend Hutchison at Emmanuel Presbyterian Church preached to his congregation: "Liberty of speech has gone mad when characters like Emma Goldman are allowed to scatter their firebrands of speech among inflammable materials like this wretch in yonder prison. Away with such as these. I would stamp the ism from our soil by driving the vessels that contain it from our shores."[13]

The *Evening News* did not forget that an anarchist enclave festered within Pierce County, twenty-six nautical miles from Tacoma, fifteen miles as the crow flies. On September 12, 1901, the newspaper boasted a banner headline: "It Is Getting Warm for Anarchists at 'Home.'" In the center of the page, a photograph showed the very boat—the Dadisman launch—that had once been seen flying a red flag. It was crowded with smiling passengers, the white streak of Abner Pope's beard visible in front and hiding his grinning mouth. The accompanying article named names. James Morton, "chief agitator," was connected to Emma Goldman and Abraham Isaak. Abner Pope described himself as a "pantarchian": "By this he means a ruler of himself." Charles Govan and *Discontent* got a mention too: "The paper is circulated widely in the United States and in many foreign countries. To be sure, the sheet has only 700 in circulation, but it is radical enough to stir up agitation wherever it goes."

"The people of Pierce County have been aroused almost to pitch of desperation by the *Evening News* sensational expose of the group of anarchists and free lovers located only a few miles from Tacoma. That such a contaminating plague spot should have flourished so long—so close at hand—flashes upon the minds of many of the people as astounding," the newspaper claimed in the opening paragraphs, making no mistake about its objectives. It did not say who these people were, nor how many there were, but nonetheless the newspaper positioned itself as the voice of the mounting hostility toward Home as it declared: "The populace is rousing itself. On every side are heard mutterings that mean nothing short of final extermination for such a reeking hell hole as that at Home."[14]

))())(

AT FIRST IT APPEARED that McKinley might survive, but after an almost week-long rally, he suddenly succumbed to infection and died on September 14. On the same day that the *Daily Ledger* printed President McKinley's last words—"Goodbye, all, goodbye. It is God's way. His will be done"—it also joined in the attack on Home. It had remained silent on the issue since the shooting, but the editors made up for the lost time with ferocity. The newspaper posed the question: What was to be done with a settlement of outlaws clearly sympathetic with the assassin? The only option appeared to be removal. "This is not to advocate violence, but to vindicate decency. There surely must be legal methods of reaching these filthy things. There is more than one charge on which they may be proceeded against. If the government of the United States has no method of reaching the traitors, the government of Pierce County is not helpless. The vile can be driven hence," the newspaper declared. "They constitute an insult to every proper instinct, and there is no reason why they should be tolerated. They despise the Constitution and thus have thrust themselves outside the pale of the Constitution. They are not citizens, but excrescences, and in the effort to purify itself Pierce County must drive them away."[15]

On the night of McKinley's death, eighty-five members of the Grand Army of the Republic gathered in the hall of the Custer post. These silver-haired fighting men closed ranks around the memory of their fallen compatriot, William McKinley, who had achieved fame during the Civil War delivering hot meals to soldiers returning from battle. Once again, duty called upon them to defend the Union. Through a resolution, they formed the Loyal League of North America. The *Daily Ledger* stated its sole objective: "The extermination of anarchy in all its various forms, by legal means if possible, and if not, by other means which will be equally effective."[16]

Over the next week, the Loyal League considered chartering a boat and sending an investigative party to Home. But other voices spoke against such a drastic measure and argued instead in favor of proceeding against the colony for those known to practice free love. "This would include most of the colony, and the members left, it is believed, would quickly scatter. At the same time, the committee holds to the belief that there are but few rabid anarchists in Home. So, while steps toward eradicating the colony will be taken, it is not likely force will be attempted."[17] On September 19, the same day that ten thousand people filled an auditorium in Tacoma to attend a memorial for McKinley, the committee opened its membership to the public. Men could sign up at McDonald's Cigar Store, and by noon, the list contained a hundred names, many of them belonging to prominent citizens of Tacoma.

‖‖

OVER THE PAST CENTURY, various journalists, writers, and scholars have recounted an aborted Loyal League raid. Certain common elements always appear in the different accounts of the story. In Tacoma, there is always a crowd of enraged, armed men—often described as three hundred strong— bent on wiping out the anarchist colony. And in Home, there is a clutch of brave, nonviolent colonists who learn of the planned raid and prepare to calmly submit to their fate. At the last minute disaster is averted when some intermediary, a Confederate soldier who lived in Home or a Tacoma minister, mollifies the Loyal League. But the best stories always involve Ed Lorenz, captain of the steamer that regularly called at Home.

Sylvia Retherford, granddaughter of one the couples who founded Home, recounts in her 1982 memoir the most dramatic depiction of the event.

> The raiding party chartered the TYCONDA on a Sunday in October to
> come to Home. Local people were forewarned and frightened, but they
> set up tables on the dock to greet their visitors with handshakes, food,
> and flowers, as this treatment had calmed other excited antagonists. This
> reception committee never did find it necessary to extend their hands across
> the tables as Captain Ed, having heard some of their fiery speeches before
> embarking, had a plan. He took the party aboard and steamed out into
> Commencement Bay, where the boat developed "motor trouble" and sat
> quietly for several hours while the angry passengers calmed down. Then,

being too late for the trip, he returned them to Tacoma and refunded their fares.[18]

I cherish the opposing images of peaceful anarchists waiting at tables decked with the bounty of the land and the raiding party cooling off on the decks of a steamer in Commencement Bay. If I let my imagination go, the tablecloths begin to flap in the same breeze that blows through the open windows of the *Tyconda*, dissipating the rank odor of angry men in wool suits. At the center is Captain Lorenz knocking around in the engine room, emerging occasionally to shrug apologetically to the frowning leaders of the Loyal League, then descending into the oily darkness. I want this version of events to be true, even though I doubt its accuracy.

None of the sources written at the time mention a possible raid, though residents of Home certainly feared one. In November of 1902, just a month after the supposed event, Oliver Verity wrote perhaps the most accurate assessment in *Discontent*. He acknowledged the danger, recalling how the abolitionist William Lloyd Garrison was once dragged through the street with a rope around his neck while his printing office burned. "That the little paper *Discontent* did not receive the same treatment accorded Garrison was not the fault of the Loyal League or its champions, the *Daily Ledger* and the *Evening News*. Just how the calamity was averted, none will probably ever know."[19] Whatever happened, the different stories reveal one fact that impressed itself on the collective memory of the residents of Home: the colony would not have survived if land instead of water connected Tacoma to Home.

)O(O(

A MINISTER FROM TACOMA, Reverend J. F. Doescher of the German Evangelical Trinity Church, did decide to personally investigate conditions in the colony. He arrived by steamer on a Wednesday late in September and stayed for two days. On Thursday evening, he lectured on religious subjects, endeavoring to teach the anarchists that there is a personal God and that Christianity is the only way that men will be truly happy, for time and eternity. Over forty people politely listened, and at the end of his talk, many came forward to shake his hand and thanked him very much for coming. Some even asked him to return.

"I visited a good many families from home to home," Doescher wrote in a statement published in the *Daily Ledger*. According to his report, the people in Home were not dangerous malcontents. He found them to be consistently cordial and intelligent people who had mysteriously come to believe in anarchism. But they assured him that not one of them expressed joy over McKinley's death. And none of their neighbors had especially grave complaints against them. The minister especially praised their industry, evident in the cleared and improved land and abundant orchards.

"I have no advice to give as to what the government should do with the anarchists," he wrote in conclusion, "but as an old man of over sixty years, and as a citizen of our beloved country, I wish to implore all my fellow citizens not to commit any unlawful act against the anarchists; let us not become anarchists ourselves in our zeal against anarchism."[20]

〉〈〉〈

ON SEPTEMBER *24, 1901,* a steam-powered launch no one had seen before motored into Joe's Bay and pulled up to the float. The passengers debarked and marched up the slope to the office of *Discontent.* There they found James Morton bent over a desk, working on the next issue. Deputy Marshall Crosby, with Postal Inspector Confucius Wayland beside him, told Morton that he had a warrant to arrest Charles Govan, James Larkin, and James Adams. A grand jury seated in Spokane, Washington, had indicted the men for the crime of writing, publishing, and mailing certain lewd, obscene, and lascivious material. Morton wondered why he was not included in the indictment; he was the editor after all, and one of the most vilified residents of Home. Marshall Crosby explained that the offending article, a criticism of monogamy and defense of free love titled "A Healthy Comparison," had been published before Morton arrived in Home. Crosby then asked Morton to identify the suspects and warned him against attempting to shield or protect them.

Morton pointed out Govan among those in the office. He then went to find Larkin and Adams, and half an hour later returned with them. "They did not evince any surprise when informed of the nature of the charge but expressed a willingness to accompany the officers to the city," reported one newspaper. "They were allowed to go home and don their best clothes and prepare for the journey."[21] While they waited, Oliver Verity invited the officers into his home for lunch and refused to accept remuneration for the meal. To take the money would violate the Golden Rule, the principle

James Adams in his
Prince Albert suit

that governed their lives in the colony, he said, but finally relented when they forced the tender upon him.

The three prisoners returned dressed in their finest clothes, with James Adams wearing his Prince Albert suit. A crowd of men, women, and children gathered on the shoreline as the men walked down to the launch and climbed aboard. As the boat pulled into the bay and motored toward Carr Inlet, the crowd shouted, "Peace, harmony, and happiness go with you."[22]

The hospitable reception made an impression on Marshall Crosby. "From their talk, and as far as I could see from their actions, the members of the colony with whom I came in contact appear to be living on a very high spiritual plane," he told the *Evening News* upon his return to Tacoma. "They deplore McKinley's assassination as deeply as anyone you would meet, and declare that murder is not the way to reform humanity and put it on a higher footing. They advocate free lovism, but with qualifications which they assert rob the theory of its degrading principles. They are emphatically the apostles of the gospel of nonresistance, and apparently their chief end in life is to live happily and peacefully together."[23]

XOXOX

ON THE SAME DAY that the *Daily Ledger* reported the arrest of the anarchists in Home, Wednesday, September 25, 1901, it gave updates on Leon Czolgosz and Emma Goldman. After a trial that lasted eight hours and twenty-six minutes, Czolgosz was found guilty. Most of the case was devoted to establishing the fact of Czolgosz's sanity. The defense presented no witnesses, and the jury delivered its verdict—guilty of murder in the first degree—in less than an hour. Two days later, Czolgosz was sentenced to death in the electric chair.

Emma Goldman, though still liable to be called "the high priestess of anarchy," fared much better. After two weeks in prison, she and her alleged co-conspirators were released for lack of evidence of any plot. In the month that followed, she would try to explain the mentality of Czolgosz. She said she did not know him, nor could she even concede that he was an anarchist, but she felt sympathy nonetheless: "He was a soul in pain, a soul that could find no abode in this cruel world of ours, a soul 'impractical,' inexpedient, lacking in caution (according to the dictum of the wise); but daring just the same, and I cannot help but bow in reverent silence before the power of such a soul, that has broken the narrow walls of its prison, and has taken a daring leap into the unknown."[24]

✕✕✕

As THEY WAITED FOR THE EVENING TRAIN to Spokane, the anarchists were held in the Chamber of Commerce building in downtown Tacoma. Larkin, who was the youngest among the prisoners, did most of the talking, telling reporters that they were not surprised by the arrest. He said that no course of action had been decided upon yet, and until they went to Spokane, he did not know what steps would be taken to secure their release. Smooth-faced Govan remained quiet and withdrawn, which the newspapers interpreted as sullen sulking. Nearly deaf, Adams composed upon his face an unfailing grin, his long whiskers concealing his lips and hanging down to his stiff lapels. That evening they were escorted to a train, and by morning the dry sagebrush country east of the Cascades was scrolling past their windows.

In Spokane, bail was set for each of the men at $1,000, the trial was scheduled to occur in Tacoma in the late winter of the following year, and the men were allowed to return to Tacoma, still in custody. They tapped friends and family for funds and soon were released.

The pages of *Discontent* began to rally support for their trial. Morton trumpeted the threat to free speech: "Popular ignorance and prejudice are the great stumbling blocks to be met and overcome. Victory or defeat will be of the utmost significance to both the friends and enemies of freedom. It means the establishment of a precedent which will either strengthen or cripple the liberty of the press. Which shall it be? Your action or indifference may decide the matter. Here is a perfectly straightforward issue, on which Liberals of every school can unite."[25] Each issue carried a statement of the facts of the case, along with a listing of the contributions to the defense fund.

With donations from organizations like the Manhattan Liberal Club and anonymous individuals all over the country, the fund began on November 11, 1902, with $95.50 and steadily grew over the following months.

As everyone waited for the trial, Home returned to its seasonal rhythms and noted the community's activities in the "Home News" section of *Discontent*. For several autumn nights, the men held lanterns above the nearby creek and snagged salmon out of the current with gaff hooks. Leonard Hicklin grew the biggest radish anyone had ever seen: it was longer than his arm and weighed as much as a year-old infant. All of the bounty was smoked or canned, put up for the winter, as darkness nibbled at the daylight. Low gray clouds drew in from the Pacific, soaking the land with various drizzles and downpours.

The weekly routine of sending out *Discontent* continued as well. A group gathered around the warm office stove to wrap the papers. They were bundled and given to Mrs. Penhallow, who then sent them out on the local steamer to Tacoma. But then Morton began getting letters from subscribers complaining that they weren't receiving issues. Oliver Verity went to the Tacoma post office to find out the reason and learned that Postal Inspector Wayland in Seattle had ordered the paper held, pending an investigation. As Verity pressed for answers, the postmaster shrugged, unable to offer an explanation: somebody higher up had made the decision. With postage paid, the back issues sat in piles, going nowhere.

Morton suggested a motive for the action: the officials wanted "to cripple the defense of our comrades, by depriving them of the assistance of *Discontent* at this critical juncture."[26] The issue of *Discontent* notifying its readers of the situation was sent out in a special wrapper. Without any indication why, this one, along with the previous issues waylaid in Tacoma, were suddenly released and filled subscribers' mailboxes with over a month's worth of *Discontent*. More and more contributions to the defense fund poured in, and by February, it had reached the desired $500, enough to cover legal expenses.

)O(O(

Postal Inspector Wayland was a busy man during the winter and spring of 1902. He kept an eye on the publications coming out of Home and wrote a series of detailed reports that he submitted to the grand jury seated in Spokane, all of them recommending some kind of action against the obscene material flowing out the Home post office. Just days before the *Discontent* trial was to begin, the grand jury responded by issuing four additional indictments. The first was a revision of the original one against Larkin, Adams, and Govan, which they considered too loosely drawn; the new indictment dropped Govan, because he was only the typesetter, and homed in on Adams and Larkin as the responsible parties. The second was for a letter Adams had mailed. The third went after Mattie Penhallow, the postmistress, and Lois Waisbrooker for the article "The Awful Fate of Fallen Women" published in *Clothed with the Sun*. The fourth and final one nailed the whole community for spewing its filth far and wide. Or in the legalese of the indictment, the "avowed anarchists and free lovers had abused the privilege of the post office establishment and department" by sending out "matter calculated to corrupt or injure members of the body politic." It recommended closing the post office.[27]

Although this new development pleased the Tacoma newspapers, not everyone was in favor. J. W. Gaskine, a frequent visitor and participant in other utopian settlements, wrote an op-ed in defense of the colony, criticizing the grand jury: "The post office at Home is not a privilege—it is a right! The American people live under a constitution and not under the despotism of an opinion." He was no believer in anarchism, though, and had just published an exposition on the value of law in the paper. "It would seem as if we were drifting toward a period of twofold tyranny—by officials and by mobs. The most confused ideas of right and wrong dispute with each other in public affairs, and we have on one side the stupidity of anarchy, proposed, and on the other the stupidity of bigots who would suppress freedom of speech which offends them. In the midst of this confusion and melee, law indeed should interpose and bring all parties to their senses."[28]

)O)O)(

BY THE DAY OF THE TRIAL, March 11, 1902, winter had loosened its grip. The defendants had left signs of the coming warmth emerging in Home. The stalks of the ferns were beginning to wilt and brown, clearing way for the fiddleheads tightly coiled inside. Nubs of swollen blossoms dotted the branches of flowering trees, soon to unfurl the first color besides evergreen on the hillside. But the weather itself contained a tincture of winter nonetheless—cool and cloudy, with a light breeze—and spring seemed far off in Tacoma. An opalescent haze of low clouds and city smoke hung outside the windows of the third floor of the Chamber of Commerce Building, where the federal court held its session.

At the front of the courtroom sat the defendants James Adams, his white beard contrasting with the dark fabric of his Prince Albert suit, and James Larkin. Beside them, their two lawyers were preparing for the case. A small crowd murmured behind them, many of them residents of Home. The red hair of James Morton could be seen in the crowd. Oliver Verity, treasurer for the defense fund, and James Govan were there too. Lois Waisbrooker, wearing a long, dark dress and holding a cane, and Mattie Penhallow had traveled from Home to hear the indictments against them and awaited news of their own trial. A mood of uncertainty ran through the voices. With the new indictments, few expected that the case would end in acquittal, and most were prepared for a protracted battle. Morton summed up the situation: "We must gird up our loins for a long and severe struggle."[29]

Postal Inspector Wayland took the stand first in the *Discontent* case. Having subscribed to the magazine, he easily identified the issue containing the offending article when the prosecuting attorney held it up and then submitted it as evidence. He also recounted a conversation he'd had with Larkin and Adams that seemed a clear admission of responsibility for the article and its publication. When the court went into recess, the defendants and their lawyers and friends dined and discussed the case and fortified themselves for the slog ahead. Even if the odds seemed insurmountable, this was a fight for free speech, a battle against laws that were so often used to arrest radicals who were discussing issues of sexuality and women's rights.

When the court reconvened, Judge Cornelius Hanford spoke from the bench before the next witness could be called forward. He said that he had carefully read the article in question over lunch and did not find it obscene or unmailable. The entire room was struck silent, and for a moment, it was quiet enough to hear the ticking of radiators and the bells of passing street cars. The defense attorney rose and quickly motioned for an acquittal. The prosecuting attorney, E. E. Cushman, vigorously opposed this move, railing against free love. Clenching a copy of *Discontent*, he read with sarcastic emphasis sections of the article in question. There were several passages that the attorney might have chosen, especially from Adams's critique of marriage: "The coarsest, filthiest and most sensual animal in human form may associate with a woman, if he be her husband, and treat her in the most brutal manner that woman can be treated by man, may infect her with sexual diseases until her whole system is filled with rottenness without damage to her virtue."[30] Whatever he selected that day, his flailing did not perturb the judge. In a calm voice, Hanford stated that in cases of this kind, the question of obscenity is ordinarily left to the jury, but this was an extraordinary case where the evidence did not support the allegations.[31]

Seated in the crowd, Morton was thrilled to hear the soundness of the judge's opinion and summarized his comments later in *Discontent*. "The passage which Mr. Cushman had read with such special emphasis contained no obscene implication, the judge said. If such an article should be held to form a legitimate basis for indictment, a vast burden would be placed on the courts in the future to select a small amount of mailable matter from the enormous quantity which was unmailable."[32] The judge sustained the motion for acquittal and instructed the jury to bring the verdict: not guilty.

The next day, nearly the entire colony filled the Adams house to celebrate the victory for free speech. Congratulations, chatter, and laughter spilled out of the guttering light of oil lamps and dissipated in the darkness beneath the trees.

✗✗✗

JUST FORTY-FOUR DAYS AFTER the assassination, Czolgosz was strapped to the electric chair and executed. Within four hours, alienists performed an autopsy, examined his brain, and confirmed that he was sane. To ensure that no one would question their findings, the source for all future doubts was entirely erased, as vividly illustrated in an article about Czolgosz in the professional journal *The Alienist and the Neurologist*: "The remains of the murderer were buried and destroyed by means of a carboy of commercial sulphuric acid poured upon the body in the lowered coffin. Thus ended the legal retribution in oblivion and extinction of every physical vestige of our good President's dastard destroyer and even his clothing and effects were burned."[33]

In the same issue of *Discontent* that described their victory, Morton picked up a little-noticed news item about the question of Czolgosz's sanity reported in the *Boston Herald*. Two physicians, Dr. Channing and Dr. Briggs, had recently released the findings of an exhaustive investigation into the life of Czolgosz. Briggs collected a wealth of information about the man from numerous friends and family members, and Channing later collated and analyzed the facts and data. When their findings were presented to their colleagues, the doctors couldn't agree on Czolgosz's sanity. Yet one thing was certain: "Dr. Briggs said positively that there was no proof that Czolgosz was an Anarchist, beyond his own statements."[34]

)O(O(

THE VERY REEL OF MICROFILM I've been using to piece together these events bears the mark of how temporary Home's victory was. As the year 1902 rolls along, the issues space out more and more. February 5, February 19, March 19. Are the holes in the run of *Discontent* the result of haphazard collecting or faulty storage? Or are they evidence of the heavy hand of the tenacious Postal Inspector Confucius Wayland? He seemed to use everything in his bureaucratic power to keep this obscene matter from polluting the general populace. The last issue on the reel, April 23, opens with an announcement titled "A New Infamy."

> Just as we are about to go to press, we learn that a dastardly blow has been struck against us, and through us, at the right and liberties of the American people. The postmaster general, without even the semblance of an investigation, has issued a ukase robbing us of our post office![35]

It says the next issue will have a full account of the matter. The closing of the post office was scheduled for April 30, 1902. On that day, the last issue of *Discontent* was mailed out, but somehow this issue didn't make it onto the reel. After April 23, the reel returns to the almost black of exposed microfilm.

)O(O(

BY THE TIME OF THE TRIAL of Lois Waisbrooker and Mattie Penhallow, the hopes of the colony were shaky. Still, a contingent of twenty people rode the steamer from Home to sit in the stuffy courtroom on that July day in 1902. When the judge entered the room, Waisbrooker lifted her thin frame in a long dark dress and leaned on her cane. Her cheeks were hollow, her brow wrinkled, but her eyes contained a sharp glint. In spite of her apparent physical weakness, she was determined to face yet another day in court. Mattie Penhallow, the former postmistress of Home, stood beside her. In her forties, she could have been Waisbrooker's daughter, but she didn't have the old woman's fortitude, and emotions played on her face as the women awaited their fate.

Jury selection took a while because so many people were already familiar with the case. Once the twelve men were selected, the trial began as the earlier one had. Postal Inspector Wayland appeared again as a witness, stating that he had subscribed to the newspaper and received the offending article. A postmaster from Ballard supported these claims. But a different judge was seated on the bench, and he didn't deliver any surprises. The long, hot day listening to testimony wore on Waisbrooker, and she eventually fainted, fell to the floor, and had to be carried out. Even though she soon revived, she was not well enough to hear the jury deliver its verdict: Penhallow, acquitted, and Waisbrooker, guilty. The highest penalty was $5,000, five years imprisonment, or both; perhaps reflecting his own ambivalence with the jury's finding, the judge fined Waisbrooker $100. This seventy-five year old woman became the only person in Home convicted of a crime as a result of the hostility that arose after the McKinley assassination.[36]

✕✕✕

RESIDENTS OF HOME MUST STILL send their mail from the Lakebay post office, but the walk is much shorter. In the 1958, the postal service decided to move the Lakebay post office to Home for ease of access. The Tacoma Narrows Bridge had recently opened, mail delivery by boat was phasing out, and the Lakebay post office was out of the way, perched on a local wharf. Its name has been a touchy subject over the years though. In the 1980s, Sylvia Retherford, who knew the history, led one group that argued for the name to be changed to Home. Another more practically minded faction didn't want to order new stationery and labels. Petitions were signed, letters were published in the local paper, someone drew an editorial cartoon of a building labeled "~~Lakebay~~ Home ~~Lakebay~~ Home Lakebay Post Office."[37] Bureaucratic inertia seems to have won out, and the post office retained its Lakebay designation.

A steady stream of trucks and cars pulls in and out of the parking lot of the post office while I sit in my car with the postcards I want to mail to my wife and son in Tacoma. I'm conducting a little experiment to find out what outgoing zip code will be stamped on cards. As I read what I've written, I feel a sudden impulse to skew the results and show my allegiance. On the top right corner of each card, next the stamp, I write: "Mailed from Home." And down at the bottom, a post script: "Sent in honor of Lois Waisbrooker." At the counter inside, I pass the cards to a bearded postal worker. I watch him closely, hoping he will notice, but he just takes my mail and tosses it into a tote.

)O(O(

THE WASHINGTON STATE LEGISLATURE did not forget how powerless everyone felt after the McKinley assassination, and in February 1903 it overwhelmingly passed one of the most virulent laws against anarchism in the nation. The new statute defined criminal anarchy as the doctrine that organized government should be overthrown by force, violence, or assassination, and it became a felony, punishable by ten years of prison or a $5,000 fine to teach, spread, or advocate the doctrines of criminal anarchy.[38]

A month or so later, in Home, James Morton started *The Demonstrator*, the newspaper that succeeded *Discontent* as the colony's organ of propaganda for the next half decade. "The cause of free speech is the cause of man. A gagged mouth is worse than a shackled body," Morton declared on the front page. "All true progress must come by the road of freedom of expression. Let us, therefore, build well for the millions who are pressing ahead, that the course might not be checked by stumbling blocks unworthy of an enlightened age."[39] But to get these words out from Home, someone had to lug the bundles of papers, carrying them by rowboat or trudging what would become a well-worn path, to the post office in Lakebay, the next town over.

Life at Home: Work

"BEING AMONG THE CHRISTIANS and feeling a little worse for the yoke, I was glad to see Olivia's reply to your comment on booming Home," Gertie Vose wrote to the editor of *The Demonstrator* in March 1904. She had been living and working in Tacoma two months, having left her son Donald in Home with relatives. "If there is anything that would have tendency to warp one's judgment in favor of our dear little land of homes, it would be a case of a seeking an opportunity to serve the plutocrats. It may be a needed step in our development. If one gets a bit out of sorts at Home just let them get outside and brush up against the powers that be."[1]

While hunting for work as a domestic servant, she had suffered "the haughty arrogance of the upper ten." They ordered her to stand, sized her up, and cross-examined her. Upon passing this gauntlet, however, she was now able to observe "the white-washed pillars of society" from within. "On the stage, how virtuous, cultured and altogether swell; in the closet the rattling of dry bones," she wrote. "I am working nights, another great advantage of our competitive system and march of intellect. The only company I have during the long night hours is roaches, rats, and mice."

Gertie may have missed Home, but for all the joys of life that could be found at Joe's Bay, paid work was not one of them. Most residents cobbled together earnings from piecemeal jobs eked out of the land or the effort of building the colony. They logged timber; they harvested huckleberries, blackberries, and other fruit; they built and improved each other's homes, sometimes for pay and other times in exchange for other services. In Home, the prevailing wage for any work, skilled or unskilled, for many years was fifteen cents an hour, but was raised to twenty cents an hour in 1903, so carpenters could keep themselves outfitted with tools.[2] Families often fed themselves off their own livestock and garden plots. The general store took money but also produce, vegetables, and work as barter.

There were a few paid positions: school teachers, owners of rooming houses, store clerks, barbers, a cobbler. For a while, the White Electric Soap factory occupied a space just south of the dock, and five-year-old Elwood ("Swede") Wayson, a local boy, appeared in their advertisements, which had the tagline: "It will all come out in the wash with White Electric Soap."[3]

It's not known how many people the company employed in Home, but the strong soap chapped the knuckles of local women as they scoured against washboards.

The butcher, John Buschi, found it a difficult place to work and was often grumpy. Some attributed his sour mood to the food fads that rippled through the colony—calf brains one moment, vegetarianism the next—but he was a gruff and brooding man by nature and seemed to bicker with everyone in the colony. The children liked to scare themselves by sneaking through the draw just south of the Jopp house up to his slaughterhouse. Hidden behind a tree, they would watch him butcher the animals, cleaving hunks of meat upon his block and tossing entrails upon the ground. In her memoir of growing up in Home, Sylvia Retherford suspected that the land here remains fertile from all the blood soaked into the soil. Buschi kept himself employed by selling meat outside the colony, to the Delano Resort and the Glen Cove Hotel.

But most people had to scavenge income outside the colony, often by moving for a while to Alaska, Oregon, Fox Island, Yakima, Seattle, or Tacoma. The "Home News" section of the colony newspapers ran announcements of the travel people took for work: "The scarcity of the 'almighty dollar' has caused Will F. Hein and Adolf Gross to go to Tacoma in search of employment."[4] Tacoma, more than any other place, was economically linked to the settlement. Gertie Vose, writing from there in 1904, found the city wanting in comparison. Too many "No Trespassing" and "Keep Off the Grass" signs hung in the city parks, and the same signs might as well have been hanging upon the brows of the stony, closed-off faces of the people she met in the street. And everyone seemed dressed in a ridiculous abundance of dry goods, attempting to look the height of fashion. A belligerent ignorance seemed to infect the crowds around Gertie, especially when they marveled at the warship *U.S.S. Tacoma* docked in port, cheered the baseball teams, and admired the preening and useless drills of the cavalry regiment. And yet Tacoma, a modest juggernaut of industry and capital compared to larger cities, was the likeliest source of the currency that circulated through Home.

Gertie Vose's time in Tacoma made her yearn for Home and abandon her characteristic sarcasm. "These lovely, soul-inspiring days, I long for dear Mother Nature's charms—the woods, the vales, and running brooks, and the songs of wild birds, in short, to wander free as the wind," she wrote.

"The ambition for gold, with all its corrupting powers, may wear the imperial robes and crowns, but give me rapturous thrill of love—love for all nature's charms.

"I guess I'll end this heterogeneous letter, written at intervals, of wool gathering. Wishing you good speed, I am yours, Gertie Vose."

CHAPTER THREE
No Spires, No Saloons

JUNE 21, 2010

WAVES SLAP AGAINST the fiberglass hull in a comforting rhythm that reminds me of lying in the bow of my father's sailboat when I was a kid, but I mustn't dally and reminisce. I've got to climb through the hatch and onto the deck. At the rail, I lean over and haul in the bumper. When it reaches my hands, the huge black thing feels awkward, as if I'm manhandling a giant penguin. Even though I grew up around boats, it's been a while since I've been on one, and the knots and protocol are distant memories. The bumper rattles its metal frame as I slide it inside.

My friend David is at the wheel inside the cabin. I found out he owns this twenty-four-foot power boat only recently. "I came into some money a little while ago," he told me with a grin. "My retirement is a jar full of pennies. And what did I do? I went ahead and bought a boat." He doesn't look like a guy who worries too much about retirement. Tall, thin, and muscular, he just entered his fifties but seems ten years younger than his age and has the enthusiasm of a man twenty years younger. I asked whether he might want to take a boat trip to Home.

Over water was how most people traveled to Home a century ago, and they usually started right here in Tacoma. Between 1900 and 1910, visitors saw what seemed to be a vibrant, if somewhat isolated community of anarchists, a rare place on the shores of Puget Sound without saloons or church spires to mark its presence. Yet when the accounts of the individual outsiders are laid on top of each other, like the sediments of a stream, they reveal traces of a decline that no one, visitors or the community alike, could see at the time. I hope that by following their route through the water a century later, I might channel what these visitors saw.

We pass beneath the Murray Morgan Bridge. This drawbridge doesn't split in the middle but was built to lift on a massive rectangular frame. Who knows the last time it was raised. Neglect and decay have forced the city to barricade its entrances with orange barrels and mesh. To some, it's an eyesore; others want to renovate it. Love or hate it, the bridge is a Tacoma landmark, impossible to ignore, especially on those clear days when the rusting hulk frames the white peak of Mount Rainier. But I can see none of this from below, as I crane my neck to examine the struts and girders. We pass quickly through the shadow of this crumbling threshold between the Thea Foss Waterway and Commencement Bay.

But no one visiting Home during the first decade of the twentieth century would have known this bridge or its name. Sure, there was the Eleventh Street Bridge, but the current drawbridge was built in 1913; and not until 1997 was it renamed in honor of local historian Murray Morgan, who chronicled the past of his hometown, Tacoma, as well as various other places in the region. And those visitors might not even have called the great peak glimmering in the distance by the name we use today. Congress created the Mount Rainier National Park in 1899, taking a cue from the British explorer George Vancouver, who designated the mountain in 1792 after his friend, a corpulent rear admiral who never actually saw his namesake. But one of the magazine articles about Home published in 1910 still referred to it as Mount Tacoma, the phonetic approximation of the native word for the peak. Some know-it-all came in later and corrected the author, crossing out "Mount Tacoma" and writing in black pen "Mount Rainier." And later still, someone, perhaps a fastidious librarian correcting the record, crossed out this "correction" and wrote in "Mount Tacoma." The mountain hovers today on the horizon, its immensity a mockery of this dispute over nomenclature.

April 12, 1900

Unlike most visitors, Roland Muirhead traced the shoreline of Key Peninsula, trudging south to Home. While in Seattle, he'd heard about the small, experimental communities in south Puget Sound, and after visiting the socialist colony of Burley, he wanted to see the anarchist colony of Home for himself. The woods were impenetrable, so he kept to the beaches, hopping and climbing over behemoth logs tossed askew upon the shoreline by tides and storms. Along the way, he passed apple and cherry trees in bloom, huckleberry and currant blossoms. Around noon he stopped and dined on a banana, a stale piece of rye bread, two figs, five pecans, and three sweets while listening to the waves lapping on the shore.

As he continued, above him rose clay bluffs from three to fifty feet high crowded with conifers. It began to rain, but the walking was easy. He was a Scotsman in his thirties, a tanner by trade, who had worked as a cowhand in South America and lived on an Owenite colony in Washington State during the 1890s. He'd returned to the United States to ramble around the West for a year. In his diary he did not say what he was looking for in Home, but as someone attracted to reform, he probably just wanted to try out this anarchist experiment for a few weeks. Here's what he did write: "Fine sloping beach all the way to Joe's Bay."[1]

His first view of Home was late in the afternoon, under low clouds. Three children were rowing a flat-bottomed boat across the silvery water of the bay. An area cleared along the shore, about fifty acres in size, held a cluster of houses constructed mostly of unpainted, rough-sawn timber. Beyond, the hills were still dark with firs. The sounds of men sawing and whacking with axes carried across the water. He inhaled the smell of freshly cut wood tinged with the smoke of several burning slash piles. Muirhead walked to Mr. Burton's house, was greeted cheerfully, and had some tea.

April 13, 1900

Muirhead filled his first day in Home with splitting wood, eating, and talking. Breakfast was modest—bread, butter, and two boiled eggs—but the midday meal, which he called dinner, consisted of a cornucopia of local fare: mashed potatoes, fried clam fritters, whole wheat bread, dried salmon, stewed dried apples, brown prunes, and berry jelly. "Very tasty set out and clean," Muirhead commented. His host introduced him to members of the colony, and as he wandered between and into their homes, he found them grubbing out roots to eat, sharing the work of erecting a house, burning tree stumps, clipping toenails.

When he returned to his room at the end of the day and described in his diary the people he'd met, he consistently described a person's physical characteristics, then noted whether he or she believed in variety, or in other words, practiced free love. Also recorded was a person's adherence to Spiritualism, a movement popular during the era that sought to communicate with the spirit world through mediums and séances. Mr. Adams: "Old man, white hair, anarchist, variety and spiritualist." Mrs. Adams: "Old lady about 65 or 70 … A lot of grandchildren. Think all are spiritualists." Mr. Penhallow: "Uncommonly prominent featured chin and nose, brow not large, dark complexion, clean shaved … Is spiritualist, but has not seen manifestations." Mrs. Penhallow: "About 40 or so, very quiet but pleasant spoken person, pale sad face, but lights up with cheerful smile when spoken to." (Apparently, the Penhallows did not practice variety.) Mr. Govan: "5 feet 4, dark complexion,

The Dadisman
family

small, thin, wiry man, clean shaven, about 40 or 50 years of age, prominent features … Does not dance. Is free lover, not married. Has been and is now printer by trade." And so on through the colony.

Sometimes his observations captured barely concealed domestic tensions. Mr. Dadisman: "Strongly built man of 40 yrs, prominent nose, fair hair brown deep set eyes, big head, probably of Dutch descent—free thinker." And Mrs. Dadisman: "A stout woman … Rather distant manner, abrupt but tends to be contrary. Seems jealous of her husband who believes in variety and is free thinker while Mrs. D is down on variety and free thought." On his visit, Muirhead toted a camera around with him. Before I came across Muirhead's diary, I had seen his photographs, and my eyes were always drawn to the raw earth beneath the colonists' feet. After reading it, I notice the tension in the photograph he took of Mr. and Mrs. Dadisman and their son Harry. Father and son look directly at the camera, the elder with his thumbs jabbed almost jauntily into his vest and Harry either scratching himself or reaching for his sleeve. Mrs. Dadisman stands slightly off balance, though, as if about to walk away, gazing out of the frame, toward the water, perhaps mildly exasperated with the Scotsman and ready to get back to the next task.

Muirhead never mentioned how he came by the information about variety, but most likely the colonists, rarely shy about their beliefs, shared it openly with him. When he met the postmaster Elum Miles, the old man did most of the talking. "Listened mostly," commented Muirhead. The small settlement was still in its infancy. The office of *Discontent* was still open. Home had not yet lost its post office, and the community's sense of itself had not hardened from the trials and publicity that were a little over a year away. They could still dream of an anarchist metropolis upon Joe's Bay. George Allen (who, by the way, did not have prominent features or practice variety) said to Muirhead, "We hope to make a large city of this place."

June 12, 2010

I climb up the ladder and take a seat on the sun deck. David steers the boat from inside the cabin, but on the console before me, there is an extra steering wheel and throttle. They move as if a ghost is at the controls. I begin jotting things in my notebook, but the panoramic view of Commencement Bay is more than my scribbles can capture.

To my right floats a tugboat moored just offshore from the enormous piles of sawdust at the Simpson Tacoma Kraft paper mill. Squatting out on a peninsula in the tide flats, the mill seems a throwback to the factories that drove the growth of this town over a century ago. Tall smokestacks eruct billowing clouds above a complex chockablock with outbuildings, towers, tubes, and pipes. With the breeze blowing, I cannot smell the pulp. Although the mill's new owners have cleaned up the production process, it is the source of what people refer to as "the Tacoma aroma," a sulfurous haze that now hangs over town only on windless days. Visitors leaving for Home certainly would have seen the mill, which has been in operation since 1890. But it is a remnant of an economy that is largely gone. Over a hundred years ago passengers on the steamer to Home would have passed a waterfront packed with sawmills, incinerators burning scrap wood, and smelters, each billowing their own smoke, creating their own aromas.

I gaze in the opposite direction, toward the city. "Tacoma is built mainly on a hill 20 to 500 feet high," wrote Muirhead when he visited. "Has fine business streets with some big blocks and electric trams long ways. Cable cars cross streets as very steep like Seattle." The electric trams and cable cars above dirt streets are long gone, though a light rail car has been running for almost a decade now in downtown Tacoma. I can't see it, though, nor the traffic downtown. Green, leafy trees, which have grown in the generations since Muirhead, obscure my view. On a Saturday morning, Muirhead and I might agree on one thing: "Not a very busy city."

Below the newer buildings, I can see some of the same buildings that he saw. The brick clock tower of the Old City Hall, built in 1893, just before the Panic burst the bubble of this boom town, still stands above the hillside. And across the street from it, the round and squat spire of the old Northern

Pacific Headquarters Building points at the sky, as it has since 1888. From its windows, the managers of the railroad company, which more than any other decided the fate of Tacoma, once took in a commanding view of the commodities arriving and departing by ship and by train. But no one looks out at me today from either vantage. Both buildings are in various stages of reincarnation: a developer wants to turn the Old City Hall into condos but is on the verge of foreclosure, and the Northern Pacific Headquarters Building is now used mostly for storage.

Along the shoreline, a forest of black pilings comes into view. As solid and permanent as these creosote-treated, barnacle-encrusted old-growth trunks appear, they seem decapitated and impotent, easy to miss and only suggestive of the docks and warehouses they once supported. I think of all the visitors who passed across the long and steep switchback of stairways to Municipal Dock. Some of them were notable in their day: anarchists Emma Goldman and Alexander Berkman, hobo poet Harry Kemp, Wobbly leaders "Big Bill" Haywood and Elizabeth Gurley Flynn. And there were the lesser-known visitors too: a "Lady of Mystery," who was never identified and spoke of friendship with Leo Tolstoy; a man named John Newman, who simply identified himself as a wanderer. And there were those who left extensive records of their visits: the Scot Eugene Muirhead, the sailor Philip Van Buskirk, the young Lucy Robins Lang, and the detective William J. Burns and his operatives. Here is where they all boarded or debarked from one of the Lorenz steamers.

"Can you take the wheel?" David shouts to me from inside the cabin. "I want to come up there." I set my notebook down and take hold of the steering wheel. The boat plows smoothly through the water, and soon David is climbing the ladder, smiling.

April 14, 1900

In the morning, Muirhead dug butter clams out of the gravel. On the tideflats, beneath a ceiling of low clouds, he dislodged one or two coin-sized clams with each thrust of his spade and soon filled an entire pail. In the afternoon, he trolled for sea trout with Harry Dadisman. "Rowed along about 20 yds from shore for hour or so but got none. Weeds stuck hook often." While out fishing, Muirhead somehow damaged the rowboat: "I broke wood from rowlock and spent time from 4 PM to 6 mending. Dadisman has handy workshop. Find everyone to be helpful and thoughtful of one another." That evening he supped on his catch of the day with Mr. Burton and commented, "Clams good flavor but a little tough."

Later that evening, Muirhead shaved his chin and went to the weekly dance in the one-room schoolhouse. Constructed of rough-sawn board, the room inside was twenty by forty feet wide, had a platform at one end decorated with flowers, blue draping, and in large letters, the word "Liberty." Here the fiddle players stood, along with a man calling out dance steps in the lamplight. "Between 40 and 50 colonists turned out from tiny children of 4 years old to people of 70 with white hair," wrote Muirhead.

> All dancing together. Many "quadrilles" but entirely different from Scotch quadrilles. I tried them but most of time looked on and talked with several of them. Many youths about 16 to 20 and girls the same age. All in good humor and not a harsh word or unseemly word spoken and most of them believe in anarchism, though all don't practice free love. I did not see any unseemly conduct. A feeling of homely intercourse.

The only refreshment was cold water. Most of the men wore black or dark clothes of various cuts, their collars starched. The women were in skirts to their boot heels and light-colored smocks, nothing gaudy or heavy. "Women invite men to dance as often as men ask women." Sometime after midnight, Muirhead walked back to his room under a calm and cool sky. "Moon obscured by clouds but lighting water of bay like silver. Trees giving clear dark shadows. All very fine to feel and see."

But even in the idyllic days of Muirhead's visit, I probe for signs of the colony's decline, early symptoms of weakness long before anyone could have imagined discord. They don't emerge until I read about Muirhead taking the steamer *Typhoon* to Tacoma. There, Muirhead bumped into the printer of *Discontent*, Charles Govan, in a bakery. They began speaking about the colony, and Govan said that he liked living in the country and would not go back to the city. Muirhead later jotted down the gist of their conversation: "Thinks colony valuable as an example to the world if it succeeds. Some objectionable people in colony, such as Fox, but can't help that, and cooperation is only voluntary." This man named Fox was not Jay Fox, who would later move to the community, but someone Muirhead describes as a fifty-year-old pensioner with a wooden leg and an eye injured in a knife fight. The implication is that he and others like him were mooching off the system. Govan asserted his firm belief in the soundness of the system: "Does not think that living apart from rest of world will hurt them mentally. Looks upon this as practical experiment."

JUNE 12, 2010
WE BOTH SIT ON THE SUN DECK, a good ten feet or so off the water, David with his hands resting on the wheel and the throttle, me with my notebook. Ahead, a line of chop curls in a long arc from shore out into the bay. Is this the ever-fluctuating line where the mocha-colored waters of the Puyallup River give way to the flat green of Puget Sound? As we passed the mouth of the Puyallup this morning, the low tide produced rapids, and so far we've been traveling through its brown effluence. Silt muddies the Puyallup, and its drainage shifts, pools, and swirls at the bottom of the bay, constantly changing with the tides. Seen from shore, it looks like an enormous emulsion, the boundary between the two immiscible liquids coiling in the logic of fractals and sea shells. I've always wanted to see it up close.

We're passing Old Town, the part of Tacoma settled first, and heading north. Where sawmills, boatyards, and warehouses once crowded the waterfront, a pleasant walkway now connects a series of parks. To the north, we can see the spit of land that held the ASARCO smelter, which once spewed arsenic-laden smog all over the region. It's now called Point Ruston, and a developer is building luxury condos on the superfund site. "Death central," David comments, when I point it out. In the distance, above an immense foreground of water and forest, rise the Olympic Mountains still patched with snow.

But my attention returns to that line in the water. The narrow ripple seems etched in the surface, with the wind rippling the water at slightly different frequencies on either side. The bow cuts through it, and the water turns green. We begin to see the pale circular smears of jellyfish floating just below the surface. How can two waters so close to each other remain so distinct?

MAY 18, 1902
"IN THE AFTERNOON, trudge over to Lake Bay to get a handful of cigars; two friendly loungers are in the store, whom I join for a round of beers," wrote the old sailor Philip Clayton Van Buskirk in his diary. "In the Home Community no tobacco nor intoxicants to be had."[2] This was his second trip in as many days to the next town over, and he would become very

familiar with the route. Almost daily, he followed the curve of Joe's Bay, strolling forty-two minutes at a leisurely pace, picking his way through swampy spots, to the place where he could briefly satiate his cravings for smoke and alcohol.

At the Seattle Public Library, Van Buskirk had read in *The Seattle Times* of the closure of the Home post office. He wrote to the colony and began a correspondence with George Allen, who invited Van Buskirk to board with his family. At seventy-eight, Van Buskirk had kept a diary for over half a century. He began writing in 1851 at the age of seventeen, and his life spent at sea, first as a marine and later as a naval officer, influenced his method of recording his life. His diary resembles a ship's log of his own emotional weather, distances traveled, and significant encounters. "Whatever I think, whatever I feel, whatever I do, whatever happens to me, I hesitate not to describe in this diary—if I have the words to do so," Van Buskirk wrote. "It is not intended that anybody, save myself, shall read these pages; that is, while I live; as to whether I will leave them after me, that is something I have yet to determine."[3]

Fortunately, he did bequeath the thirty-five volumes to a relative, who donated them in 1905 to the University of Washington Libraries. Hand-ruled lines form borders across the headers and margins where the date and place of the entries are noted. The writing itself is in a neat and readable cursive with few misspellings or crossings out, as if copied from a first draft. Flipping through the pages, reading the orderly lines, inhaling the sour smell of the bindings, I sense that this enormous document was the closest thing to a home the itinerant sailor had. When he stepped off the steamer in Home in 1902, he had been living in Washington for a couple of decades and had failed to find a wife and settle down, as he had hoped he would when he retired from the Navy.

In his first couple of days in Home, he had met most of the residents and listened to musical performances in the Allen's house. He was seeing the community less than a month after it had lost the post office and had an opportunity to witness firsthand their response to this event, but it receives only two sentences: "Mrs. Penhallow was postmistress til the 30th ultimo when the Home office was discontinued. Since then the Home settlers use the Lake Bay post office a mile and half distant, a messenger being sent every other day for the mail and distribution to the settlers being done as before by Mrs. Penhallow and her husband."[4]

The fresh air, the hospitality, the wholesome life of these anarchists only stoked his ache for intoxicants. At the end of each month, he drew a table and in it listed expenses, the places he stayed, what he read, acquaintances newly made, letters received, and health problems. On this page, in May 1902, he noted: "Pestered with decaying teeth and an abominable repulsive mouth." And the next page over, the only trace of an internal conflict about his frequent trips to Lakebay to buy cigars: "Breach of tobacco pledge."

MAY 1902

AT THE END OF EACH MONTH, Van Buskirk also compiled a list of his activities, boiling each day down to a single event. At the end of May 1902, he sat in his guest room in the Allens' house and neatly compressed his stay in Home into seventeen lines, a snippet of which captures how he didn't quite fit into the anarchist colony:

21. The Allens have a new boarder.
22. Mr. Verity and I have a little spat.
23. Hear Mr. Morton read from Shelley.
24. Little or no meat at the Allens.
  * Visitors come to see what "anarchists" look like.
26. Evening with Mr. Verity.
27. These days frequently to Lake Bay—for cigars.
28. Our new boarder leaves us.
29. Again hear Mr. Morton read from the Poets.

These were the facts that Van Buskirk carried away in his journal, where they jostled against each other like so many bones collected in a bag. Some were commonplace, such as the boarder he met, named Mr. W. Cloerfield, who lived at 109 Yesler Way, Seattle, and had briefly stayed with the Allens for reasons that Van Buskirk does not explain. But most of them pointed to his growing dissatisfaction with the place. Not only did Home lack intoxicants, it didn't have much meat either. Only once during his stay did he taste flesh: chicken on a Sunday evening.

He didn't get along with the colonists either. He had quarreled not just with Oliver Verity but also with his host, George Allen. On May 22, he wrote, "Had quite a little spat with Mr. Verity and another with Mr. Allen. I guess I started both spats being nettled by the persistent use of the terms 'thief,' 'bloodsucker,' and 'vampire,' also 'parasite,' whenever allusion is made to those classes in the Nation whose members are not actual and manual laborers." The colonists were probably a little testy after losing the post office, but this man who had roamed the world and known the protocols and hierarchy of military life could not countenance such a simplistic view of things. After tempers cooled, he seems to have made up with Verity, since he visited him only a few days later.

He also did not appreciate the sight of James F. Morton, Jr., whose readings he considered tedious and all too frequent. The list doesn't quite capture his reluctant attendance on May 29: "In the dusk of evening call to have talk with Mr. Penhallow, only to be trapped into listening to another reading of the Poets (this time Wordsworth) by Mr. Morton." The audience was the same as the week before, three women, "with addition of Mr. Penhallow who, however, needing rest from the labors of the day, soon fell asleep."

Van Buskirk drew red stars next to certain days. There was probably some rhyme or reason to it, but I couldn't tease out a pattern in the short time I viewed the diaries. I don't know why the visitors from Tacoma got a star. Did he find them amusing? Petty? Ridiculous? The sentences written on May 25 don't elucidate much: "Two strangers come in the same boat; dine with us, and will depart for Tacoma later in the afternoon. Their visit is only to see what 'anarchists' and 'free lovers' look like." These two anonymous tourists would have found that the Allen family didn't look out of the ordinary. A photograph of Mrs. Allen and the four girls, taken around this time, shows them as their guests might have seen them. The way the older girls, Grace and Leila, squint out of this picture, aware of being watched by a device

Sylvia Allen and her
daughters

that can record their image, is not altogether different from how Home was beginning to view itself. The anonymous guests who attended dinner on May 25 were just drops in the stream of visitors that passed through Home after the McKinley assassination. All of the publicity had firmly put the town on the map as a curiosity, and even if Van Buskirk condescended to the gawking and probably disappointed tourists, he had been drawn by the same forces.

June 12, 2010

At Point Defiance Park, the shoreline becomes heavily forested with Douglas fir. Commander Charles Wilkes named this place when he passed through on an expedition in the 1840s, observing that the high, narrow peninsula could provide an excellent strategic defense for Puget Sound. President Andrew Johnson set it aside as a military reservation in 1866, protecting this land from almost certain clear cut and development. In 1888, Grover Cleveland transferred ownership of the property to Tacoma, which turned it into a city park. On maps, this verdant bit of land looks like the neck of a geoduck clam extending out of the grid of city streets to the south. It is perhaps one of the few spots where I can glimpse some of the same trees that the numerous visitors to Home saw from the handrails of the steamer.

But my eyes don't stay long on the trees. Ahead is an obstacle course of boats floating in a haphazard pattern between Point Defiance and Vashon Island. We see a sea lion poke up from below, his pudgy body briefly rolling just above the surface, then submerging, probably going after the same salmon these boats are fishing for. David navigates between the small craft bristling with fishing poles.

"Catching anything?" he yells as we pass close.

"Just small guys," one of the fishermen yells back.

To our left stretches Owen Beach, a swath of gravel and driftwood, empty even though it's late morning on a Saturday. Then, as we reach the horn of Point Defiance, the jagged rim of the forest presses in, clinging to bluffs that drop nearly straight down to the beach. A large green lamp on metal struts marks the end of the land, and just offshore from it, directly in our path, the water becomes strangely flat. Waves disturb the water all around us, but here some bottom feature presses the tidal flow upward, creating a smooth circle on the surface a good thirty feet in diameter. David steers the boat right through, taking a hard left and turning the boat south into the Tacoma Narrows. From here on, things will be less familiar.

JUNE 2, 1902

"WITH EYES OPEN yet seeing nothing. Limbs sound yet doing nothing—spiritless, indeed more dead than alive," wrote Van Buskirk soon after he returned to Tacoma. While in Home, he'd harbored cravings that neither tobacco nor alcohol could slake, and as soon as he got back to the city he sampled the temptations of the flesh available for hire in Opera Alley. As he gave in to his urges, conflicted and self-loathing, his powers of description only increased:

> Between half-past five and six p.m., I enter what looks from the outside to be a well-kept, high-class house of ill-fame. Find inside three inmates (the whole crew)—all three mulattos, one very dark. I feel like backing out at once, but hesitate, tarry a little, and at last choose at a venture, the dark one, as the least forbidding. All illusions vanish when we reach her dirty little room, and have disrobed. Good-natured and chatty but for the rest, big, fat, and it seems scarred all over, this most repulsive creature. Her name, she says, is Clara Jackson, the state she came from Kentucky, and her age nineteen—more likely twenty-three. It is too late now for retreat.

He performs the sex act—"a vile copulation," he calls it—which leaves him feeling cheaper and meaner than when he arrived.

I had read of Van Buskirk's visit in the history books, and much of what I'd found in his diaries—the frequent trips to Lakebay, the spat with Verity and Allen, the complaints about food—did not surprise me, but I had somehow forgotten the mention that his first activity after leaving the colony was to visit a whorehouse. As tantalizing as this is, and as much as it reveals about Van Buskirk's loneliness, I cannot help but wish that he'd encountered something in Home that set his heart clashing with itself like the dalliance with Clara Jackson did. This entry is longer and more detailed than any single entry he wrote while visiting the anarchists, and he devotes more lines to Clara Jackson than any individual he met on Joe's Bay.

But Van Buskirk's primary interest was not Home, its residents, or even the historical record. It was his own life, with all its quirks and habits, the biggest one being his constant ordering of experiences into the pages of a diary. "Hasten to bath and change my underclothes, lest some germs of disease may have been brought away from the dark mulatto's crib," he wrote. Even if he did not feel clean and refreshed, seeing this night logged and recorded must have provided some relief. The next day he would wake and mail four boxes of candy to Home, a good-bye present for each of George Allen's daughters, but first he had to get through another night alone with himself and his diaries.

JUNE 12, 2010

THE BOAT TROLLS ALONG, the bow pounding the waves, the wake spreading in swells behind us. On either side rise the tall bluffs of the Tacoma Narrows. Here the water of the Puget Sound presses through a crease less than a mile wide, generating intense tidal currents. I had briefly considered kayaking from Tacoma to Home but changed my mind when I went for a walk at Titlow Beach and saw the current charging like rapids out of the Narrows.

The Narrows is a convergence zone of powerful forces, and the wind can roar through here, too. There are two suspension bridges ahead of us, connecting Tacoma to the Gig Peninsula and points beyond. On the closest, cars pulse across the span, heading west. This bridge replaced one that collapsed in 1940. The grainy black-and-white footage of a bridge gyrating in the wind, concrete and steel oscillating like slender ribbon, is perhaps the only iconic image Tacoma has produced. In the weeks before it fell, locals flocked to watch "Galloping Gertie" twist in the November gales, many of them carrying cameras. As we approach the bridge, I'm thinking about something in the periphery of those photographs, noticed perhaps because I live here: the slopes on either side of the Narrows were dark, almost black with conifers.

Now houses perch on the ridges, and on the Tacoma side, they seem stacked on top of each other, all positioned to take in views of the bridges and the water. The bridge that replaced Galloping Gertie opened in 1950, and it fundamentally changed how people traveled in these parts. Before, the peninsulas were almost as isolated as islands, only accessible by boat, but afterward, concrete and steel stitched them to the city. As more and more people moved over, commuters, many of whom waited in three- to four-hour backups, wanted an even stronger connection. Another bridge was built and opened in 2007 to carry eastbound traffic.

The shadows of the bridges lie in dark stripes on the water. We quickly pass through them, then beneath the bridges themselves. I look up through the mesh at the underside of the vehicles. That could be me up there; that's how I usually get to Home.

May or June, 1910

As THE PADDLEWHEEL STEAMER pulled into Joe's Bay, Lucy Robins Lang and her husband, Bob, stood at the rail and sighted their first view of the colony: a little white cottage with blue trim out on a point. Then, more cottages with small gardens and fruit trees appeared. Lucy wondered what it would be like to raise a family in such a rustic place as Home. She and Bob had lived in Chicago, New York, and San Francisco, and as they talked of trying their hand at farming, perhaps they nurtured the rosy, bucolic visions of country life that many city dwellers have.

The ship passed a stretch of native forest, the towering trees and thicket of brush a reminder of the immense wilderness out of which this small community had been hacked. Then the hillside opened up. Lang could see the buildings of the community spread across the slope. "The colony was a crazy quilt of tents, shacks, and neat cottages," she later wrote in her memoir.[5]

By her mid-twenties, she had already experienced much. She was born in Russia; her family immigrated to the United States when she was nine and eventually settled in Chicago. She began working in a cigar factory, and as a teen was exposed to the radical political ideas pulsing through urban centers and energizing many sensitive, intelligent young people. She gravitated toward the anarchists and met her future husband, Bob Robins, in the Waldheim Cemetery—the spiritual center of the radical world in America, she called it. On trim paths, beneath the shadows of the trees, a short distance from the statue on the tomb of the Haymarket martyrs, she and Bob flirted with each other. They eloped when she was still in her teen years.

In her memoir, *Tomorrow is Beautiful,* she opens the chapter that recounts her visit to Joe's Bay with these sentences: "Together again, Bob and I set out for Home Colony on the shores of Puget Sound. Now that our marriage had been tested, we wanted children, and we wanted the right environment in which to bring them up." The "test" she mentions wasn't the typical challenge of fidelity or hardship. Rather, she and Bob had specifically arranged to have a "trial marriage." Although Lang acknowledged and respected the principles of free love, she observed that women in these relationships, especially when they became pregnant, often still ended up shouldering the burdens of traditional relationships. To avoid such a situation, she and Bob drew up a legally binding contract that stipulated that household tasks would be shared, that there would be no children, and that the marriage would automatically become annulled at the agreed-upon duration of five years.

They signed the contract and spent five happy years together, mingling with the likes of Emma Goldman and Jack London and running a cigar store in New York and a vegetarian restaurant in San Francisco. They amicably separated when the time came, even though Bob preferred not to. When the San Francisco press got wind of the scandalous arrangement, a brief but intense flurry of denunciations raged in the newspapers. In spite of the bad publicity, some admired Lang's unconventional approach to marriage, but she turned down invitations to speak to women's groups. "I hadn't advocated and wasn't interested in advocating a trial marriage for everybody; I simply tried to make a workable plan for Bob and me."

Reunited, they would now try the simple life in Home. As the boat pulled into the wharf, their friends Ida and Mike Rubenstein from Chicago were on the dock waiting for them. The new arrivals weaved their way around the freight, bales of hay, sacks of bran and meal, and boxes of canned goods and went down the gangplank. The old friends embraced and then climbed the hill to the Rubenstein's large five-room house. Mike made his living as a tailor in Tacoma, and his salary allowed them to live more comfortably than many of the colonists. While touring the Rubenstein's home, the friends entered a room with a view of Mount Rainier hovering like a mirage, its peak bejeweled with snow even though it was early summer. Whenever Lucy and Bob saw the mountain framed in this window, they felt that they should remain in Home for the rest of their lives.

July 4, 1910

THE SMELLS OF ROASTING CHICKEN, fresh bread, and baking blackberry pies filled the air around Home on Independence Day. Colonists were busily preparing for a group of picnickers arriving from Seattle and Tacoma.

Progress had slowly and quietly touched Home in the first decade of the twentieth century. The community had grown to just over two hundred people and now covered the hillside. The colonists had celebrated their tenth anniversary in 1906, and *The Demonstrator* (the newspaper that had replaced *Discontent*) had chugged along for several years, until it put out its last issue in 1907. The colonists had made many improvements. They finished the wharf, so that people could now walk out to the boat landing. They cut and leveled roads on the slope of the hill. They built and improved their houses. One significant achievement was the construction of Liberty Hall. It was a two-story, unpainted structure with a school room and a printing office on the ground floor. The second floor had a large open space where colony functions were held: dances, evening talks, and other social gatherings. From all points around the colony, trails twisted around blackened, stubborn stumps and led through brush to this gathering place. Just outside the hall, on the morning of July 4, 1910, they decorated picnic tables with flowers and hung pictures of heroes of the radical world: Karl Marx, Peter Kropotkin, and Michael Bakunin. "We wanted our visitors to see the portraits on the wall and to realize that this was no bourgeois institution but the abode of free spirits," wrote Lucy.

They had sold tickets for a fundraiser to revive the colony newspaper. Jay Fox, a prominent anarchist from Chicago, was now living in Home and intended to start a paper called *The Agitator*. Everyone was in a festive mood as they set the tables. The sounds of firecrackers set off in Lakebay traveled across the water as if they were exploding right there in Home.

June 12, 2010

THE WATER HAS CHANGED colors again, this time becoming a deep steel blue. I didn't notice exactly when it happened, but it was somewhere in Hale Passage that the surface took on the sheen of calm that gives the illusion that Puget Sound is a large alpine lake rather than a body of water haunted by tidal forces and strange currents.

Enormous houses squat on the ridgelines of the land on either side, their many large windows aimed toward the water. On Fox Island, the houses are mostly tucked into the woods, but on the Gig Peninsula side, they are all painted gray or beige and crowded into subdivisions with manicured lawns. The neighborhood looks like the kind of community that has a gate at its entrance and rules about how long the grass can grow and whether residents can use lawn ornaments. It's hard to imagine the residents of this community pouring out of their homes to gather at a place like Liberty Hall for an evening of singing and dancing. Perhaps because it reminds me of places where I grew up, I pull out my camera for the first time today and take a photograph.

JULY 4, 1910

AS THE ADULTS WERE PUTTING the finishing touches on the table dressings and decorations, they heard the footfalls and jeers of a rowdy crowd of teenagers running on the paths toward Liberty Hall. Cheeks red, upper lips beaded with sweat, the youngsters swerved around the blackened stumps, the brush, the picnic tables, and their own parents. They rushed right up to the clapboard walls of Liberty Hall and began yanking down the portraits of the revolutionaries. *Down with Bakunin! Down with Kropotkin! Down with Marx!* In her description of this event, Lang never mentions whether the teens were laughing or not, but I expect that they snickered at their vandalism. The parents were too shocked to stop them, and perhaps out of principle, they wouldn't have done so anyway. Where the revolutionaries had hung, the teens tacked up pictures of George Washington and Theodore Roosevelt. They unfurled a large American flag and fastened that to the wall. Cackling still, they then tore the revolutionary portraits to bits.

The parents could do nothing. The children had timed their raid to coincide with the docking of the boat. Visitors were already climbing up the hill, chatting happily and eager for food. How the afternoon went isn't mentioned in Lang's memoir, but the gracious hosts were probably as hospitable as possible. As they served their guests roasted chicken, baked bread, and blackberry pie, the adults had to hold their tongues, wondering why the children pulled such a prank.

Not until later that evening, after all the visitors had left, did the children explain themselves. They did not hesitate to speak up, initially blaming it on a seventeen-year-old malcontent named Donald Vose, whose mother, Gertie, had moved to Home a few years earlier.

Home Colony
Picnic outside
Liberty Hall

"Donald told us to do it," one youth said, his voice cracking with angst and uncertainty. "We don't want European pictures. They have American pictures in schools."

"We didn't want the people from the boat to see the foreign pictures. They'd call us greenhorns," another told his parents.

"The fellows in the other towns won't let us on the ball teams. They say you spit on the flag." As the children spoke in a chorus, it became apparent that Donald had merely found a release for sentiments that were simmering below the surface.

"Yeah, they call us bastards …"

"We're Americans. We want a regular Fourth."

"We don't wanna be crackpots. We don't wanna be bastards."

Being called bastards must have stung some of the children sorely, the vague epithet becoming precise and hurtful. A number of them, like Donald Vose, were the offspring of free-love unions and being raised by single mothers. They fit the actual definition of bastard: "a child begotten and born out of wedlock," according to the 1913 *Webster's Revised Unabridged Dictionary.*[6] As the parents attempted to shuck tradition, dreamed of an ideal society, and debated how to bring it about, some of their children nurtured anger against them. Having been raised in what their parents thought was freedom, the children were dissatisfied and wanted something else, something more conventional. Might this be a clue to the demise of Home? How could the experiment succeed if the next generation didn't share the values of their parents?

As Lang listened to the children's complaints, she felt conflicted: "Remembering my own rages against the traditions of an older generation, I could not fail to sympathize with them, but I was sorry for their parents."[7] This event contributed to her growing disillusionment with the colony and the idea of raising children there. It clearly wasn't the foothold to the future life she imagined, and by November, she and Bob would be glad to leave.

JUNE 12, 2010

WITH HALE PASSAGE JUST BEHIND US, the wooded shoreline of the Gig Peninsula stretches up the east side of Carr Inlet to the right. Across the water is the equally wooded shoreline of the Key Peninsula and our destination. From this distance, the dark boughs of the conifers dominate, concealing houses. We have a problem though: we can't see the entrance to Joe's Bay. It should be right ahead of us.

Down in the cabin, David at the wheel and me beside him, we alternate between looking at our position on the GPS and comparing it to the navigational chart that is sprawled and flopping over the edges of the table. On the GPS, bright green lines on a field of black approximate the landforms around us. A target, also bright green, locates our position, and a straight line shows where we'll end up if we maintain our course. There are two little coves, neither of them labeled. I bring the chart over. The Key Peninsula was so named because topographically it looks like an old-fashioned key hanging off the lower end of the Kitsap Peninsula. Our destination, Joe's Bay (which is called Von Geldern Cove on the chart), is the first of several notches on the bottom side of the key.

But from here, the shore appears to be a continuous thatch of trees. I suggest that perhaps the rocky point on the southern mouth of the bay obstructs the view. We determine that the best thing to do is aim the boat toward the little wrinkle on the computer screen. We climb back up to the sun deck and watch the land get closer.

NOVEMBER 5, 1910

TWO MEN OUTFITTED FOR SURVEYING WORK were standing on the porch of their boarding house when they eyed Jay Fox descending toward the landing with a bundle of correspondence. He handed it to a teenage girl, who in turn gave it to a woman, probably her mother, as they waited for the steamer to arrive. The woman put them in a valise. "As it was evident that Fox is sending mail outside of the Lakebay post office, I decided to keep them under surveillance," wrote one of the men later that day.[8] He ambled down the hill and joined the small group on the wharf waiting for the steamer, keeping his distance from the woman with the valise.

Lucy Robins Lang had seen these two men in late November wandering around Home with transit and tripod, plumb bob and compass, measuring sticks and maps, notebooks and pens, but they seemed commonplace enough in those days that she dismissed them. Her dog, Toy, barked wildly at them, though, and she had to restrain the miniature poodle from nipping at their ankles. "Later I learned that Toy was right in distrusting these men, for they were agents of William J. Burns."[9] Neither she nor anyone in Home knew it at the time, but the instruments meant to measure and record parcels of land were a disguise to help the operatives of the Burns Detective Agency infiltrate and investigate the residents of Home.

Just a month before, a massive explosion had destroyed the *Los Angeles Times* building, killing twenty people. The newspaper's owner, Harrison Gray Otis, was engaged in a dispute with labor unions over the control of industry in Los Angeles. Union saboteurs were suspected, and the city hired Detective William J. Burns for the case. "I have always insisted that every criminal leaves a track—that many times Providence interferes to uncover the footprints left by the criminal," wrote Burns in his memoir about the investigation.[10] He had traced the dynamite to a San Francisco supplier, and this in turn pointed to the address of a house rented by David Caplan—"a notorious anarchist," according to Burns. "Caplan had a wife. Both were known and had lived in the Anarchist settlement of Home colony." By sending his operatives to Home, Burns hoped to nudge Providence along.

In his account of their stay, Burns revived some of the rhetoric of the McKinley era prosecutions, calling it "the nest of anarchy in the United States." Numerous errors mar his account. Some, such as repeated and inaccurate dates on his operatives' reports, derive from carelessness. Others seem more self-serving, such as his claim that twelve hundred people lived in Home, when in fact the colony was less than a quarter that size. Overall, he portrays a place that seems much sexier and more dangerous than it was. "They exist in a state of free love, are notoriously unfaithful to their mates thus chosen and are so crooked that even in this class of rogues there does not seem to be any hint of honor." The post office, he avers, was taken away because they celebrated McKinley's assassination with a debauch.

Burns set up shop first in Tacoma and then much closer in Lakebay, and began receiving reports from his men, which he later published nearly in full in his memoir. The operatives mostly trailed Jay Fox, who was a known associate of Caplan. Although these dispatches are colored with bias, written in clunky language, and possess an air of sometimes comical cloak and dagger, they record unique details of the lives of people in Home, especially Jay Fox.

On this November day, Assistant Manager C. J. S. shadowed the woman with Fox's mail until she deposited it in a mailbox near the Olympic Hotel in Tacoma and noted that the packages had the return address: "Agitator,

Lake Bay, Wash." How he had retrieved the items and got this information he does not say, but tampering with mail was probably a standard trick of the trade. The detectives had, coincidentally, visited the colony when Jay Fox was putting out the inaugural issue of *The Agitator*, the first newspaper to be published in Home in three years. The envelopes most likely contained correspondence about subscriptions or submissions.

The other man, Inspector H. J. L., stayed in Home that day. He went to speak to a fellow referred to in reports as *Mr. Blank*, whom they learned "was bitterly opposed to Jay Fox and his associates." The operatives were grooming him to become an informant for the agency, especially since he conveniently lived near Fox. Blank told the inspector: "Fox is a free lover; the woman with him a Jewess. They have two children—a girl about 14 and a boy about 12 years." The inspector had met the children just the night before, when they came to the boarding house to sell copies of *The Agitator*. He had bought one and gleaned from it that "Fox took part in the Haymarket riot."

Overall he was pleased with how things were going. "We are getting acquainted very nicely, going along very slowly and feeling our way and the cover is first class," he reported to Burns. "We have created no suspicion."

November 12, 1910
The operatives observed the comings and goings of many individuals, many of whom verified Burns's view of the depraved state of the colony. A certain "D." stepped off the steamer, decorated with buttons for the Western Federation of Miners and the Industrial Workers of the World, toting a trunk with all his belongings, stating that he was an anarchist and planned to stay a day or maybe a month; but the operatives believed he was just a "faker" looking for some "free love." Mrs. B., the woman who had carried Fox's letter on their first day in the colony, was a divorced Englishwoman who rented a house and "stays two or three days out of a week here, and while here, she and others of the 'free love' faith hold a drunken carnival."

Folks noticed the operatives pretending to be surveyors, too. Detective Burns himself wandered through the hills dressed as a hunter, and one resident remembered him knocking on her door in the guise of a book salesman who seemed more interested in peering around her shoulder, into her house, than selling his wares. At the time, most colonists probably just shrugged off these inquisitive strangers.[11]

Home, viewed from the water in 1910

Mr. Blank was the person they got to know best. In an abandoned cabin near his own house, he repeated for Burns a conversation he had with E., one of the storekeepers in Home. E. had confided to Mr. Blank that he had a secret he wished to tell. At the word "secret," the detectives must have leaned in close to hear what Blank had to say.

E., it seems, feared for Fox's safety. "Fox was going in with some fellows on a dangerous job and the consequence would be that Fox would get caught and be made to suffer, while the others would go free." This information seems a fever dream, a whispered rumor, words that Burns wants to hear, and Blank continued: "Fox at the time was in a hard way financially, being so hard-pressed for cash that he had to have E. extend a line of credit to him for a sack of flour." Blank went on, attempting to further implicate Fox in the bombing of the *Los Angeles Times* building. In August, a Jew came to visit and was with Fox constantly. Fox traveled to San Francisco with this mysterious man, and then on October 6, returned alone. Blank saw him on the steamer and reported that Fox had bloodshot eyes and looked very worried. But when Fox returned to Home, he suddenly had funds to repay his credit and produce the first issue of *The Agitator*.

As with most of Burns's intelligence about Home, the details of Blank's story could easily be read another way. And even these facts, which barely qualify as circumstantial evidence, could themselves be fabricated. But I am not so much interested in the insinuation about Fox's involvement in the crime as I am fascinated by Blank himself, sitting with Burns and his operatives in an abandoned cabin. Faceless, anonymous, a cipher, Blank represents the ultimate fact of how much Home had changed. It is hard to

imagine a neighbor turning on his neighbor like this in the colony's early days. Such an act violated the core principle of the community—to mind your own business.

Even as Blank divulges his secrets, he keeps another to himself, a secret that he can't speak because he isn't even aware of it. He knows Home in its decline and will perhaps participate in the dismantling of the experiment. Even as the men speak, they don't notice the creepers and vines, mildew and moss climbing up the cabin walls, devouring the damp wood, tugging the whole structure back into the earth at a speed human eyes cannot detect.

JUNE 12, 2010
"*THAT'S ABOUT AS FAR* as we can go," David says and idles the engine. "I don't want to get any closer than that."

The bay has opened up, its entrance concealed behind a narrow point that juts to the north. The tide is so low that we can't enter the bay or even approach the boat ramp. We float a hundred yards from the exposed bottom. The seaweed flattened against the worn rocks is a bright emerald against the dark water. "Oh well," I reply, a little disappointed that we can't get closer. "This is good enough for me. I just wanted to see Home from the water."

We climb back on the sun deck and start eating lunch. I pull out an old photograph of Home, the panorama published with J. W. Gaskine's 1910 article about the colony, and show it to David. The most striking difference, which we notice immediately, is the trees. In the photograph, the old growth is gone from the hillside, and only a ghostly fringe remains on the ridgeline.

Trees now blanket the hillside, and about halfway up the hill, conifers crowd around the houses, concealing all but their front facades. About the only similarity between this moment and the photograph is the calm, glassy water upon which we float.

When we finish eating, David goes below decks and fires the engine. I'm not ready to leave, but we have no reason to stay. I've wanted to travel the distance to Home over the water for so long that I want to stay a while, floating before it and savoring the view. For David, I realize, this was just the destination, and now it's getting late.

I descend the ladder and enter the cabin. "I'm going to swim to shore," I tell David.

"Really?"

"Yes. I can't resist jumping in the water."

He laughs and says, "Let me get the camera, so that I can prove you did it." Now in my swim trunks, I climb the rail, throw my arms above my head, and dive. David takes a photograph, freezing an image of me in midair, between the boat and water, arms extended, chest crisscrossed with bands of light reflecting off the water. Then the dark chill surrounds me. Most people think that Puget Sound, which usually hovers around fifty degrees year-round, is too frigid for swimming, alleging that in fifteen minutes hypothermia sets in. Perhaps because the sun has warmed the surface, today the cold doesn't so much bite as gnaw on my body as I stroke as quickly as I can toward land. In the shallows, the water warms even more and becomes clotted with seaweed. It brushes against my legs and feet as I climb out of the water and look around.

The rocky bottom of the bay, smelling of rotting fish, extends before me. I consider running the additional hundred yards or so to the boat landing just so I can say that I set foot in Home, but out of consideration for David, I just stand there, fortifying myself for the distance I have to swim back. He snaps another picture.

NOVEMBER *15, 1910*

FROM THE EARLY HOURS, when the sun first lit the hillside, Investigator H. J. L. waited in the loft of Blank's barn. It had an excellent view of Fox's home, and he watched and listened in the shadows of the barn, waiting for a clue.

Blank was now actively collaborating with the Burns men. Whether this resident of Home received remuneration for his services goes unmentioned in *The Masked War*. It wouldn't have been unheard of for him to be compensated, and if he was, the funds would have come right out of Burns's own pocket. The detective was now footing the bill for the entire investigation. While in Home, he had learned that the city of Los Angeles would not pay him until he showed results. If he gave up now, though, Burns might lose the trail, so he borrowed money, betting on a big score. Yet the best he could do was shadow Fox, who seemed to not be doing anything suspicious. Perhaps this was why Burns exaggerated when he concluded his last report from the nest of anarchy with the claim that it showed "how close we were to the heart of this colony of law-hating people."

From his perch in the loft, H. J. L. noted:

9:00 a.m.—Mail carrier arrived—left mail in box.

9:15 a.m.—A. arrived at Fox's home.

9:50 a.m.—Mrs. ———— arrived at Fox's home.

10:05 a.m.—Mrs. ———— left Fox's home.

10:40 a.m.—Fox came to mailbox, then started in a hurry toward the ———— home. Informant trailed him and reported that Fox walked around the block, hurriedly opened one of the letters, looked at it for a few seconds and then returned home.

10:45 a.m.—Mrs. ———— arrived at Fox's home.

11:05 a.m.—Mrs. ———— left Fox's home.

The log of Jay Fox's activities continues in a similar way through the rest of the day, giving a rare glimpse into a single day in the colony for Jay Fox. Mrs. ———— called on Fox four times. All morning, hammers banged and saws snored as Fox and comrade A. worked on the addition he was putting on the house. Both stopped working when A. left at 1:10 p.m. Fox wrote prolifically on such topics as anarchism, labor issues, and other lofty matters in *The Agitator* and other publications, but he rarely mentioned the quotidian details of his life. Burns deserves thanks for footing the bill to chronicle the minutiae of a day in the life of Jay Fox.

"5:30 p.m.—Man, 5 feet 8 inches, 155 pounds, arrived with two packages. It was getting dark and neither informant nor I could identify him as being anyone living in the Colony. At 5:30 p.m. this party left."[12] At dusk, Blank and Assistant Manager C. J. S. joined H. J. L. and they moved into the timber to watch the house. They stayed there until almost midnight, standing in the darkness, watching the lamplight glow in the windows of

Life at Home: Leisure

IN THEIR FREE TIME the people of Home occupied their curious minds with various pursuits. They studied Esperanto, Hatha-Yoga, vegetarianism, eugenics, fasting, and German and Oriental philosophies. They established a local library filled with works of literary and political interest. They practiced Spiritualism, held séances, and performed slate writing in individual homes. One Spiritualist group met three times a week at the residence of Mary Parker, the owner of a successful poultry business.

They recognized too the joys of sport and formed a baseball team. At the first game, the boys beat the men twenty-two to twenty-one. Then Home played against a nearby town and lost twenty-four to fourteen. When the team played in Steilacoom, inmates from Western State Hospital for the Insane sat bareheaded in the stands and watched the games under supervision. On one occasion, a resident of Home was almost locked up because he wasn't wearing a hat and the guard mistook him for an inmate.

Music provided constant entertainment in Home. Residents organized bands, singing groups, and a hodgepodge of musicians called the Home orchestra. "We received our band instruments last week—and we are tickled," one player wrote. "The cows are becoming ashamed by their inability to bawl."[1] An inventory of musical instruments in the colony a few years later counted three pianos, eight organs, eight violins, six guitars, two mandolins, two cornets, one flute, and a half dozen harmonicas.

And how they danced, especially at celebrations. At her silver anniversary, Mrs. Adams, in her eighties, stepped a lively quadrille. And in February 1906, they commemorated the ten-year anniversary of the experiment at Home. All three founders were there, and "different members talked about old times and new," marveling at how the community had grown to fifty houses and a hundred and fifty residents, all united by the idea of freedom.[2] At midnight, a luncheon was served and dancing feet scuffed and pounded the floorboards of Liberty Hall until the wee hours.

But most of their spare time was spent listening to talks at Liberty Hall and other venues in Home. Sometimes the speakers were famous anarchists and labor leaders who had addressed massive crowds and been at the center of storms of media attention. To these rabble rousers and free speech fighters—Elizabeth Gurley Flynn, Emma Goldman, Alexander Berkman, or "Big Bill" Haywood—Home was a brief respite from a busy life, a place rarely remembered later in autobiographies. For the people of Home, their brief stays were a reminder that Home was connected to a larger movement.

One of the most memorable speakers was Elbert Hubbard, founder of the Roycroft community, near Buffalo, New York. His talk was praised in *The Demonstrator*: "Only by doing something for one another, he showed, do we strengthen ourselves, and win true success in life."[3] For his part, Hubbard admired the community too: "A more intelligent lot of men and women I never saw. They have a schoolhouse and an assembly room, and here they meet several times a week to have music, to listen to an address, or to dance and spend the hour in social intercourse. I noticed that most of these people ate no meat, many drank neither tea nor coffee, a few used tobacco, but none ever use intoxicants."[4]

Home's residents listened to each other too. James Morton, Jr., ascended the stage frequently and lectured on an eclectic range of topics: "The Relation of Art to Life," "Evolution," "Primitive Man," and many more. Lois Waisbrooker spoke about women's issues and sexuality. Mattie Penhallow asked whether suffering strengthened character. Others led discussions, lyceums, and reading circles.

Many visiting speakers espoused ideas that reflected oddball trends and crazes. A woman from Tacoma accompanied her talk on astrology, phrenology, and palmistry with stereopticon slides. A representative from the Koreshanity sect posited that the Earth resided in the center of a hollow sphere and that the most direct way to China was straight up. And a man calling himself Professor Thompson stood before them in women's attire and extolled the sanitary virtues of female garb for all sexes. Some may have smirked at the way his beard rustled against his dress, but they believed that every idea deserved its airing and thus were inclined to hear him out.

The following day Professor Thompson, still wearing a dress, offered to help finish building Liberty Hall. He quickly discovered the limits of his philosophy: feminine apparel was ill suited for carpentry work. The day after that, he reappeared in a pair of borrowed overalls. People could not help from laughing and ribbing him about his new outfit. Professor Thompson remained in work clothes for the rest of his brief stay and left a memory of a man who handled crochet needles with the dexterity of a woman.[5]

CHAPTER FOUR

Crowning an Agitator

WITH LITTLE OF THE SYRUPY SHADE beneath fir trees to be found on the hillside above Joe's Bay, June and July of 1911 lay long and hot upon the rooftops. Many colonists escaped into the chill of Puget Sound. Some wore underclothes. Others stripped to "nature's garments" as they called it in those days. The frigid saltwater didn't mind what they wore. It accepted bodies young and old, supple and frail, thin and portly, pale and swarthy, clothed and unclothed.

Most folks in Home didn't care whether their neighbors wore suitable covering or not. "To the outside world Home is a colony of cranks," was how Jay Fox described the place in the inaugural issue of *The Agitator*, the anarchist newspaper he had established there in the fall of 1910. "'Crank' is a very convenient term with which to brand those who don't follow the calf path of convention. In reality it is a colony of very sensible people who mind their own business to a greater extent, and therefore are not quite so busy as the residents of other communities in which we have lived."[1]

But even as Fox published these words, some in Home did not share his views. For a time, these residents were anonymous among the two hundred and thirteen people living in Home, but around the time the rhododendron blooms withered in the record-breaking heat wave of 1911, they made themselves known by paying attention to what their neighbors were doing in Joe's Bay.

Most of the facts about the nude bathing cases were questioned and debated into uncertainty. It's difficult to determine exactly what happened, or how many times it happened. Did Anton Zoncanelli wear breeches made of a flour sack or nothing at all? Was Stella Thorndale actually seeking a saltwater cure for her rheumatism and just getting dressed when they caught her? Had Adrian Wilbers donned swimming trunks or "garments as unsubstantial as a dream," as Judge Graham later put it?

For certain, there were bathers and there were watchers. The bathers dunked themselves with a gasp and emerged with white flesh gleaming. A distance away, above the rocky shore, stood the watchers, sometimes concealed in the brush and other times perched on a mound for a better view. Then, in the early summer of 1911, the watchers began to do more than just watch: they began to call upon Deputy Sheriff Jim Tillman, who in turn arrested the bathers for indecent exposure.

✕✕✕

THIS MEDDLING IN OTHERS' AFFAIRS infuriated Jay Fox. He was not inclined to quietly suffer fools and their injustices, petty or otherwise. By the time he moved to Home in 1910, he was well known among anarchists in Chicago. Forty years old, with a head of prematurely gray hair, Fox had a narrow chin, high cheekbones, and a brow that often furrowed and concealed his eyes in shadow. "Jay had more fibre and calmness and strength than the rank and file anarchists," wrote the journalist Hutchins Hapgood. "He talks well, and reasons, not emotionally, but coolly; and in character he is balanced, tolerant and kind. He is a learned man among them, schoolmasterly in his look, and talks in a slow, deliberate way."[2] Fox came to Home hoping that it would be an inexpensive place to live and publish an anarchist newspaper.

Fox's common-law wife, Esther Abramowitz, and her two children from a previous marriage to a dentist joined him in Home. Born in Russia, Abramowitz had worked in a garment factory and then immigrated to the United States in the 1890s. With dark hair and features, she was strikingly beautiful. Her close-lipped smile contrasted a lingering sadness that seemed to sculpt her face. To contemporaries she was "voluptuous, sensual, melancholy," and "Oriental"—this last adjective because she was a Russian Jew and seemed exotic. Hapgood commented on the couple: "They have great respect for one another. Jay is so tolerant that Esther's 'longings' are completely satisfied, even when they lead her away from Jay for weeks at a time. But Jay's soul is fortified and tested: he is not emotionally vulnerable, like the poor Free Baptist publisher."[3]

Home had been without a newspaper since *The Demonstrator* ceased publication in 1907, and *The Agitator* consciously filled this gap. Compared to previous newspapers published in Home, however, *The Agitator* rarely reported on colony affairs, at least at first. Coming out every other week, it sought a national readership and contained articles about the Industrial Workers of the World and other labor unions, published political tracts of Fox's friends and associates, and summarized developments in the labor and anarchist movements in a front-page column called "The Passing Show."

"*The Agitator* aims to be a live issue, and it's going to stir things up," declared the first issue. "Its first attempt will be that of arousing comrades and friends of freedom. There is no use dallying any longer in the philosophical mazes of contemplation. We must 'dig' and do."[4] This sentiment was largely devoted to the outside world, but with his neighbors getting arrested, Fox felt compelled to stir things up in Home.

His response to the situation was an opinion piece titled "The Nude and the Prudes," published in the July 1, 1911, issue of *The Agitator*. "Clothes are made to protect the body, not hide it," he declared in the opening sentence. "The mind that associates impurity with the human body is itself impure." And he continued in this vein, attacking those in the community that would enforce their own values upon their neighbors:

> The vulgar mind sees its own reflection in everything it views. Pollution cannot escape pollution and the polluted mind that sees its own reflection in the nude body of a fellow being and arises in early morning to enjoy the vulgar feast, and then calls on the law to punish innocent victims whose clean bodies aroused savage instincts, is not fit company for civilized people and should be avoided.
>
> Home is a community of free spirits, who came out into the woods to escape the polluted atmosphere of priest-ridden, conventional society. One of the liberties was the privilege to bathe in evening dress, or with merely the clothes that nature gave them, just as they chose.
>
> No one went rubbernecking to see which suit a person wore, who sought the purifying waters of the bay. Surely it was nobody's business. All were sufficiently pure minded to see no vulgarity, no suggestion of anything vile or indecent in the thought or the sight of nature's masterpiece uncovered.
>
> But eventually a few prudes got into the community and proceeded in the brutal, unneighborly way of the outside world to suppress the people's freedom. They had four persons arrested on the charge of "indecent exposure." One woman, the mother of two small children, was sent to jail. The one man arrested will also serve a term in prison. And the perpetrators of this vile action wonder why they are boycotted.

Explicit rules for how people should behave were anathema to the anarchist experiment at Home, but the watchers had violated the unspoken expectations of its members. Not only did they not mind their own business, they had enforced their values upon their neighbors. Fox advocated the only sensible form of censure to those who did not believe in overt coercion: a boycott.

"There is no possible middle ground on which a libertarian can escape taking part in the freedom of Home," continued Fox.

> There is no half way. Those who refuse to aid the defense are aiding the
> other side. For those who want liberty and will not fight for it are parasites
> and do not deserve freedom. Those who are indifferent to the invasion,
> who can see an innocent woman torn from the side of her children and
> packed off to jail and are not moved to action, cannot be counted among
> the rebels of authority. Their place is with the enemy.[5]

)O(O(

TO UNDERSTAND WHY JAY FOX was so uncompromising in his fight for freedom, I go to the place thousands of miles away that forged his consciousness as a radical: Haymarket Square in Chicago. A large statue on the sidewalk of North Des Plaines Street commemorates what happened here. From a distance, the whole thing appears to be sculpted of red clay, but it is actually formed of steel. Out of a cement pedestal, figures lift boards and the wheels of a cart, creating a provisional platform upon which a speaker stands gripping a sheet of paper in one hand. His other hand is raised in a posture of oratory or rebuke. The figure faces the tall buildings downtown, just barely visible in the distance, and it is from that direction, I imagine, that the police came.

For Jay Fox, the chain of events that led to Haymarket had begun several days before. He was sixteen years old, working at the Malleable Iron Works, and a new member of the Knights of Labor when a general strike was called to protest for an eight-hour work day. On May 1, 1886, Fox joined thirty thousand workers picketing across Chicago. With the factories quiet, the haze that normally hung over the city cleared and revealed a broad blue sky. According to Lucy Robins Lang, Fox would carry a vivid memory of this moment: "He could draw a beautiful picture of the general strike—no turning wheels, no clanging hammers, no smoking factory chimneys—and sometimes I felt he loved the idea of the general strike because it would be so restful."[6] Briefly, it seemed the strikers might achieve their demands.

But on May 3, Fox walked over from the Malleable Iron Works, where things were quiet, to the McCormick Reaper Works. There a bonfire was burning in the midst of an unruly crowd. Strikers had captured buses carrying scabs to the factory and set them ablaze. Stones began to fly at the policemen guarding the gate. When reinforcements arrived, the officers— nearly two hundred strong—advanced and began beating the strikers with clubs and firing upon them. "As an 'innocent onlooker,' I was badly scared when a bullet plowed thru my coat, carrying a portion of my finger with it on its journey to the breast of a striker that stood directly behind me," Fox recalled. Fox pulled him to safety, but it was too late, the man died from his wound, "leaving behind a penniless wife and five small children to weep and curse the fate that brought them to 'free' America."[7]

The bullet destroyed more than Fox's finger: he began to see America as a place where freedom did not apply equally to everyone. For poor and working people, freedom was something that could only be placed in quotation marks, and as Fox stood outside the shack and watched the worker's family grieve over his body, he felt, perhaps for the first time, the fierce urge to dismantle the system that made the quotation marks necessary.

The following night, on May 4, 1886, three thousand people gathered in Haymarket Square to hear Albert Parsons and other labor leaders voice their outrage over the violence at the McCormick works. As the speeches continued for hours and the night grew chilly, the crowd thinned. Then, in the late hours, seemingly without provocation, a cordon of police stormed the square. An officer commanded the speaker, Samuel Fielden, to step off the oxcart and ordered the crowd to disperse. Just as Fielden was climbing down, someone cast a bomb, a flaming bundle that haphazardly tumbled end-over-end into the ranks of navy wool coats and brass buttons. A concussive blast lit the brick walls of the square, and then in the darkness that followed, the terrified police began to shoot indiscriminately into the crowd and at each other. In all, seven policemen died that night.

I want to place Fox there, a skinny sixteen-year-old scrambling in the melee, his wounded finger bandaged, but none of his writings about the Haymarket affair read like first-person accounts. Ultimately, whether he was physically present is beside the point: for him, as for many radicals of his generation, Haymarket and the events that followed became a passion story of martyrdom to which he was devoted with a religious fervor and a template through which he comprehended all future conflicts with authority.

"The identity and the affiliation of the person who threw the bomb have never been determined, but this anonymous act had many victims," explains a plaque affixed to the memorial, and with this Fox would agree. Ignoring due process, the justice system acted swiftly upon the assumption that the anarchists were to blame. Eight prominent labor leaders were arrested and tried, and in Fox's opinion, the industrialists and their allies simply seized an opportunity "to rid the community of eight dangerous men; men whom the glare of gold could not silence; men of proven ability as organizers of the discontented; men whose teachings were far-reaching and deep-rooted, the practical application of which would destroy every privilege enjoyed by the rich and powerful."[8]

Four of the eight men—Albert Parsons, August Spies, Adolph Fischer, and George Engel—received death sentences not for the crime, but for inciting it in their speeches and writing. After the execution, Fox walked in the massive funeral procession that followed the horse-drawn hearses carrying the red-draped coffins of the Haymarket martyrs.

As I circle the sculpture where the oxcart once stood, I feel the distance of more than a century between myself and the events that happened here. Garbage trucks, taxis, and cyclists pass on the one-way street. Most of the square itself has been converted into gravel parking lots for lofts and office spaces in the renovated brick buildings. Yet I find evidence that for some this remains a living memorial: two carnations, red and black, rest upon the pedestal, and an "A" with a circle around it, the symbol of anarchism, is drawn over the city's seal.

)O(O(

WITHIN HOME, "The Nude and the Prudes" article blasted the already fragile community into factions: the Nudes and the Prudes. In doing so, it contributed to the cycle of reprisal that had started earlier that summer. The Nudes bathed in even greater numbers, and the Prudes continued to summon sheriff Tillman, but now a principle—the very liberty at the heart of the colony—was at stake.

The first nude bathing trial in late July 1911 revealed just how high tempers were running. A schoolhouse in nearby Longbranch served as a makeshift courtroom. Deputy Prosecutor Grover C. Nolte, an attorney in his early twenties, arrived around noon on the steamer from Tacoma, and the proceedings began at 1:30 on a sultry afternoon.

"I saw Mrs. Thorndale in the water with a little girl," Edgar Hicklin—a Prude—testified. "Neither she nor the girl had any clothes on." He said that he had observed the incident while he and Theodore Meyer, son of the Home storekeeper, were strolling down a country road on the morning of July 14.

Rodger Meakins, the attorney from Seattle representing the Nudes, suggested that perhaps the two men had gone down that country road for the purpose of being shocked. Hicklin's answer went unrecorded, but he likely denied such an insinuation. "Persons possessed of enormous virtue who do not like the community better get out of it!" Meakins railed, and the Nudes burst into applause.

On the stand, Stella Thorndale explained that her doctor had ordered saltwater baths for her rheumatism, and being lame, she had asked for help getting dressed after her bath. Even though several women of Home—Anna Marquis, Bessie Levine, Gertie Vose, and Sarah Voglanoff—substantiated her claim, Thorndale was fined $65. "It should have been $100!" a Prude shouted. This comment so enraged Frank Pease, a former soldier who lived in Home, that he slugged the man. The two exchanged blows, with Pease appearing to have the advantage, until Deputy Prosecutor Nolte threw himself between the two men. People of Home shook their fists at the lawyer, saying they'd never gotten a square deal in the courts and never expected it.

Anna Falkoff and Stella Rosnick were also fined. However, Ethel Ostroff's case was thrown out because witnesses couldn't agree whether she was bathing in the nude, at a picnic, or ill in bed.[9] The trial dragged on for eleven hours, though the afternoon and into the night. Gloom crept unnoticed into the schoolhouse as Nudes, Prudes, legal arbiters, and curious bystanders waited for decisions that would only be appealed.

✕✕✕

OUTSIDE OF HOME, the authorities took notice of "The Nude and the Prudes" as well, and one evening in August a deputy sheriff arrived from Tacoma to arrest Jay Fox. Found at an evening gathering, the editor willingly gave himself up and quietly followed the officer down to the launch tied at the wharf. Fox had suspected the authorities might come for him, having read of their intentions in a Tacoma newspaper. Besides, he expected that sooner or later his writing might land him in jail: "Every radical editor is subject to such prosecution, for the powers that be are sensitive to criticism, and will endeavor on every opportunity to throttle the voice of truth."[10]

For several weeks, Deputy Prosecutor Nolte had been pushing for the arrest of Fox under the Washington state law that made it a misdemeanor to publish, distribute, or circulate any printed matter "which shall tend to encourage or advocate disrespect of the law or for any court or courts of justice."[11] The Washington State Legislature passed a version of this statute with anarchists in mind soon after President McKinley's assassination. It lay like an unused crosscut saw for almost a decade, gathering rust but with many sharp teeth, until Nolte proposed applying it to Jay Fox. Some of his colleagues doubted the statue's legal efficacy, however, and according to one Tacoma newspaper, Nolte waited for two weeks as city officials "withheld the filing until more authorities could be looked up."[12] But then someone from Home, perhaps a disgruntled Prude, tipped off the prosecuting attorney that Fox might abscond. Thus, after getting a hastily written warrant, the deputy sheriff rented a launch and arrested him in the middle of the night.

)(X)(

THE MASSIVE STONE EDIFICE of the Pierce County Courthouse once dominated the hill above Tacoma. It was built in the eclectic, ornate style of the late nineteenth century, but just like its medieval forebears, the stone façade of this Romanesque Revival courthouse exuded permanence, weight, power, and rigidity. Even the things that seemed light about the building—the arched windows, the sloped and plentiful gables, the conical roofs topped with spires, the two-hundred-and-twenty-two-foot-tall clock tower—accentuated the heaviness of the rusticated walls.

Somewhere in the basement of this building, Jay Fox was locked up the day after his arrest. Bail had been set for $1,000, but Fox's friends were only able to find Washington State Senator Peder Jenson to stand as a surety. Judge William O. Chapman wanted at least one other person. According to the newspapers, Fox's face displayed not a tremor of emotion when he heard that he would remain in jail.

As Fox waited through the night in the hardened steel tank reserved for desperate criminals, he must have remembered the other times he'd been jailed. After McKinley's assassination, he had been among many radicals across the country who were detained and then released when no connection was found between them and the assassin, Leon Czolgosz. He must have remembered too the Haymarket martyrs who had been arrested, tried, and executed for what they said and believed a quarter century before.

Etching of statue in Waldheim Cemetery in the first issue of *The Agitator.*

The first issue of *The Agitator* had been dedicated to their memories. The front page was emblazoned with an etching of the monument that marks the graves of the Haymarket martyrs in Waldheim Cemetery near Chicago. A woman wrapped in a cloak stands above a fallen man, her hand reaching toward his bearded face, her right hand angling across her body in a gesture that is bold and protective. On the pedestal are the last words of August Spies, spoken as he stood beside his comrades on the gallows, a white gown draped over his clothes, a cloth sack over his head, a noose around his neck:

"There will come a time when our silence will be more powerful than the voices you strangle today."

Jay Fox matured in this silence. *The Agitator* was an agent of this silence. As he waited through the night, confined by rock and stone and steel, Fox listened hard to this silence.

〤〤〤

THE SAME DAY THAT FOX was sent to jail, in another room of the Pierce County Courthouse, the nude bathing trials began in earnest. Anton Zoncanelli went first. Judge Frank Graham and a jury of six men heard his case. Colonel James J. Anderson, a prominent Democrat in Pierce County and a veteran of the Confederate Army, defended Zoncanelli while Deputy Prosecutor Nolte represented the state. "Many witnesses—men, women, and children—were examined on both sides. The question hinged on whether or not Zoncanelli wore a pair of white trunks or breeches made of a flour sack, instead of the mere perpetual garb donated by nature."[13]

The conflicting testimony befuddled the jury, and by 10:30 p.m., they had failed to reach a verdict. The case was thrown out due to the hung jury.

Unable to convict Zoncanelli, Nolte tried a different tack in the next nude bathing case, which began the following day. He objected to using the same jury for Adrian Wilbers's trial, and against the vehement protests of defense attorney Anderson, Judge Graham dismissed the wavering, indecisive men. Graham would decide the case alone. Witnesses testified that Wilbers swam in nothing but water, while Wilbers maintained that he was covered, just not enough to suit his accusers. With no jury to slow the process, Graham easily convicted Wilbers of indecent exposure, fining him $100 and court costs. Handing down his decision, Graham said the nude bathers of Home had worn "garments as unsubstantial as a dream and unfit for the purpose intended."[14] Unable to pay the fine, Wilbers was sentenced to sixty-four days in jail, which his attorney promptly appealed.

)O)O(

WHEN JAY FOX'S TRIAL BEGAN in January 1912, Tacoma newspapers had varying degrees of interest. Populist and pro-labor, *The Tacoma Times* ran coverage sympathetic to Fox on the front page, above the fold. Other Tacoma newspapers, such as the *Tacoma Daily Tribune* and *The Tacoma Daily Ledger*, buried stories several pages in. Perhaps indicating an editorial opinion about the significance of this trial, one update in the *Tacoma Daily Tribune* was published directly below an article titled "Only Girl to Ride Ostrich."

If some of Tacoma's newspapers were ambivalent, residents of Home were drawn to this latest and most dramatic manifestation of the nude bathing conflict. Nudes and Prudes alike were piled, perhaps uncomfortably close together, on benches in the gallery behind Fox, listening to the ticking steam heat or staring out the windows at the gray smudges of rain clouds as the court proceedings progressed.

The prosecuting attorneys for the state, Grover C. Nolte and August O. Burmeister, both young and ambitious lawyers at the beginning of their careers, needed to convince the jury that Jay Fox's intent in writing "The Nude and the Prudes" was to encourage disrespect for the law. They also had to demonstrate that the article did in fact encourage disrespect for the law, and their primary source of evidence was the purported increase in nude bathing that followed its publication. Fox's attorney, Colonel Anderson, with his pince-nez and grizzled walrus mustache, would create as many obstacles as he could. Whenever the prosecutors attempted a line of questioning that might establish any of these facts, he was prepared to stand and spit out a line that would appear like a refrain in the court transcripts: "I object to that as incompetent, irrelevant, and immaterial."[15]

For the Nudes, Jay Fox was a defender not only of free speech but of the freedom vital to the experiment at Home. Most of the Prudes were there as witnesses against Fox, ready to unload their barely veiled contempt. By January 1912, an internecine feud was roiling in Home, and Fox's trial only added torque to the conflict. The cycle of reprisal had become dynamic and self-perpetuating, with each side inflicting and receiving wounds from which the community would never recover. The Nudes continued to boycott the Prudes, refusing to conduct business transactions with them. The Prudes retaliated with violence: they physically assaulted Nudes in the street, cut down their orchards, tore down a fence, and blew a shack off its foundation.[16] Children were sucked into the fight. A girl was given an obscene note by one of her classmates, and her parent (a Prude) demanded the resignation of school teacher George Allen (a Nude). Another Prude blamed Allen for the teasing his thirteen-year-old received from his classmates, claiming that the teacher encouraged a lawless atmosphere.

Around the time that one of the chief witnesses for the state, Deputy Sheriff Jim Tillman, appeared in court, some Nudes in Home were complaining to his boss, Sheriff Longmire, and requesting he be replaced by someone more sympathetic to their views. They even had a few names, if he was interested.[17]

✕✕✕

WHEN HE TOOK THE STAND on January 12, however, Jim Tillman could still call himself Deputy Sheriff. Early in Tillman's testimony, Prosecutor Nolte asked whether he had had any conversations with Fox about the prosecution of indecent exposures in Home. Colonel Anderson objected as usual. All of the previous day, Anderson had repeatedly stymied any line of questioning about Jay Fox's intent with his vociferous objections, but this time, Nolte was prepared to explain his reason for the question. Tillman sat there stiffly while Nolte turned to the judge and spoke:

If it was shown that he edited that article, we also have a right to show the intent he was imbued with at the time he edited it, and the best way in the world is to show what statements he made in regard to the subject matter of the editorial. If he made any statements which would explain it, we would certainly have a right to show it as bearing upon the proposition of intent. If his intent was to encourage disrespect for law, if he showed any disrespect for law previously, the jury has right to take that into consideration.

But Judge Chapman would not permit this attempt to establish intent. "What a person who writes an article may have said at some previous time is of little assistance to us in determining the effect of an article afterwards written. The article must speak for itself," Chapman stated. "It does not make so much difference what was in his mind, the test is what comes out of it."

The prosecuting attorneys attempted several times to convince the judge to change his mind, but Chapman refused every time. "He may have thought that he was publishing an article that would revolutionize government," Chapman said, "but if, as a matter of fact, he did not succeed in giving expression to anything which in any degree would have a tendency to accomplish that effect, or produced that effect in the mind of any man, he should not be punished for it."

Tillman never answered the question about whether he talked to Fox about the persecution of the nude bathers, but he confirmed that there were more indecent exposure convictions after the article was published. "Do you know why there were more afterwards than before?" asked Nolte.

"They were prompted to it," Tillman said.

"By what?"

"By agitation."

"I move that that answer be stricken!" said Anderson, but Chapman didn't see how he could do that.

"Tell this jury what this agitation was," Nolte prompted.

"It was by newspaper print and talk." Nolte inquired whether there was more disrespect for the law after the article was written, and Tillman replied, "There was."

During cross-examination, Anderson immediately picked up where Nolte left off, asking, "How do you know there was, Mr. Tillman?"

"From my observation."

"You paid particular attention, did you?"

"Yes, I know from being called in as officer, and was for more than a year or two."

"You were watching particularly?"

"No, sir, I did not."

"How do you know?"

"When I go to work mornings, I take the boat, and see them as high as four or five. Never seen before so many."

"Did it ever occur to you, Mr. Tillman, that it might have been on account of the weather being warmer after the article was printed than before?" Tillman denied Anderson's point about the weather: during the two summers he'd lived in Home, he hadn't noticed any changes. "You have shown considerable enmity toward this defendant, Mr. Fox, haven't you?" Anderson asked.

"I have been investigating Mr. Fox for a year or something of that kind personally."

"What is the answer?"

"I say as man to man I haven't anything particular against Mr. Fox or his propaganda."

"Didn't you make a statement to Mrs. Minnie Smith to the effect that you would see Jay Fox hung before you left Home Colony?"

"I did not."

"Did you make any remark of that nature to Mrs. Minnie Smith?"

"I would not be positive, I think I made a certain remark to Minnie Smith that I was liable to see Jay Fox behind bars before I left Home colony, which I did. I think I made some remark about that; I never made the remark that I would see him hung."

"You have been exerting yourself about putting him behind bars, haven't you?"

"Not exerting myself at all, not as much as I should have done."

"What is there you could have done or should have done that you have not done?"

"That is my secret." [18]

)O(O(

FOX HIMSELF DID NOT APPEAR as a witness, but he was permitted to rise and directly address the jury as part of the closing arguments. Standing tall and slim in his black suit before the jury, he reiterated that his article was only intended to denounce the methods of anti-colony members of the community, not to encourage law breaking. "Don't read anything into the story that isn't there," he admonished the jury. "The court instructed you that nude bathing is in itself no violation of the law unless it is accompanied by indecent exposure, and if you, as jurors, can find one line, or word even, in this article that encourages or incites indecent exposure, then you are bound to find the defendant in the case guilty."

The judge had told Fox that he could not testify in his address, so he was in the unusual position of having to speak about himself in the third person, but Fox could not help from slipping into the first person: "I don't see why I should be singled out for writing a moderate article like that. Compared with some of the articles in the daily papers, you will find it is very modest and moderate." Attempting to articulate what guided his work as a writer and editor, he declared, "It is only by agitation that the laws of the land are made better. It is only by agitation that reforms have been brought about in the world. If the waters of the bay were not agitated, it would become a polluted pool and would soon kill us all. Show me the country where there is the most tyranny and I will show you the country where there is no free speech. This country was settled on that right—the right to free speech."[19]

In his closing argument, Colonel Anderson expanded on these ideas. "Fox criticized the laws," he told the jury. "So does every newspaper in the country. Why doesn't the state go after *The Times*, *The Ledger*, and other newspapers? They all print matter criticizing our laws, our tariff laws, the recall and others. The prosecutors don't haul them into court because there is too much power, too many votes behind them." The crowded courtroom burst into applause, and the judge banged his gavel for silence.[20]

When Nolte made his closing argument, he didn't touch the free speech issue. Instead, he dredged up old biases against the anarchists and Home itself. "The State of Washington was organized long before Home colony was. The laws were fixed here long before Home colony was founded," stated Nolte. His sense of time was a little compressed—Washington became a state in 1889, and Home was founded only seven years later—but such details didn't weigh down the flight of his rhetoric. His cheeks flushed, he exclaimed, "They knew that this state was an organized society at this time, and if they didn't like it, why did they come here? They didn't want that liberty which is the liberty that means freedom under law and order; they wanted that kind of liberty that gives them the right to do as they damn please!" Getting carried away, he repeated this phrase again: "They want to do as they damn please!"

"Mr. Nolte, I think you may cut out one or two of those words," chided Judge Chapman, and Nolte apologized. Judge Chapman instructed the jury that the defendant was not being tried because he was an anarchist or advocated nude bathing, unless it was indecent exposure. He also enumerated the guarantees of free speech, but said that this didn't mean that the press could be used as "an engine for evil and designing men to cherish for malicious purposes, sedition, irreligion and impunity." Further, he defined disrespect for the law not as a specific disrespect but as disrespect for law in general or law as the basis of government. Criticizing a particular law didn't justify finding the author guilty. The jurors—ten men and two women—took these instructions and all the testimony and arguments that were spoken before them into the jury deliberation room.

✕✕✕

ON THE HUNDREDTH ANNIVERSARY of the verdict in Jay Fox's case, I visit the site of the Pierce County Courthouse and find in the back corner of a parking lot, above moss-covered asphalt, an obscure plaque commemorating the building. "The County Courthouse was the original occupant of this lot. The stone wall is all that remains of the historic structure," reads a marker affixed to the very wall it describes. Looking like the last remnant of a dungeon, the rough sandstone blocks, darkened with spots of lichen, run the length of the lot. Boarded-over passageways lead below the imposing brick structure of the National Guard Armory just up the hill. "The courthouse was demolished in 1959. It was considered a fire hazard."

When the wrecking ball smashed through the walls, it exposed sunlight upon the jury room where the ten men and two women deliberated over the fate of Jay Fox. They sat somewhere thirty feet or so above my head. They had not reached a decision by ten o'clock on the night the trial ended, and they continued into the second day. Did some take Judge Chapman's words to heart and puzzle over the principles of free speech? Did others simply want to damn that anarchist to clink? They took so long that people outside began to whisper that the trial might end with a hung jury, but they finally emerged at five o'clock on January 12, 1912.

"Guilty of the crime of editing printed matter tending to encourage and advocate disrespect for the law, as charged in the information," spoke the forewoman, Lida Kenewell, the wife of a wheelwright at Griffen Wheel Company. Perhaps indicating that this decision was not reached with the same certitude as a steel wheel rolling upon its rail, she added: "We, the jury, ask leniency of the court."

Excused by the judge, they filed quickly out of the courtroom. Colonel Anderson rushed forward, seeking an explanation from the jury. "There's your verdict—that's all we have to say," one of them said.[21]

Today, a century later, two National Guardsmen in the alley behind the Armory are loading machine guns into the back of a white delivery truck, chatting nonchalantly and handling the weapons as if they are cordwood. An attorney in a dark suit parks his car without glancing up and briskly walks to his appointment in the huge block of concrete, glass, and steel that replaced the old courthouse. The weather is cool and clear, fogging my breath and chilling my hands, and as I leave the lot, I see that the attendant ensconced warmly in his booth wears only shirt sleeves. I notice too for the first time that, just beyond the beige building of C. J. Bail Bonds, Mount Rainier is visible. At least once, Jay Fox, upon emerging from the courthouse and descending its front steps, could have squinted upon the bright immensity of the mountain. The white dome, the first sight of the outside world, would have ached in his eyes.

)O(O(

CHIEF WITNESS FOR THE STATE, Deputy Sheriff J. M. Tillman lost his job on the Saturday immediately following the jury's verdict. "Owing to the factional quarrel that has existed in Lakebay and the Home colony for some time I am obliged to cancel your commission as a deputy sheriff," wrote his boss Sheriff Longmire in a letter. Tillman handed over his star and told a visiting reporter he was on the warpath: "I am footloose now, and I am going to fix the parties that done the job."[22] How or whether he carried out his vengeful intentions goes unrecorded.

Soon afterward, the retrials of the nude bathing cases were heard in Pierce County Superior Court, with Judge Chapman again presiding. The same attorneys as in Fox's trial assumed familiar roles: Nolte and Burmeister prosecuting, Colonel Anderson for the defense. By now the interest of the newspapers was tepid, as if the proceedings were just a worn out vaudeville act. Only *The Tacoma Times* reported much of the farce, describing how several members of the Geitman family testified that they had seen Adrian Wilbers bath nude. None could agree on the distance, however: Della claimed she watched from two hundred feet, but her teenage daughter Lillian thought it was only a hundred, while little Charlie, only nine, testified that they had climbed on a mound to get a better view.[23]

The trial ended with a hung jury, and perhaps seeing that doubtful evidence might swamp their other cases, the prosecutors dropped charges against Anna Falkoff, Stella Rosnick, Stella Thorndale, and Anton Zoncanelli. The whole community celebrated in Home, and Zoncanelli, normally a respectable and mild-mannered bachelor, was so overjoyed with his acquittal that he drank too much beer and insisted that all of the beautiful girls kiss and dance with him. He had to be escorted away from Liberty Hall for the evening.[24]

)O(O(

SITTING AT HIS DESK for the first time since the trial, Jay Fox breathed the familiar odors of his office: damp paper, ink, and oil upon the joints of the presses. Rain dripped off the eaves of Liberty Hall, splashing on the saturated ground outside the window. Behind him, just beyond the small clamshell press for handbills, squatted the massive wooden frame of the hand press used for *The Agitator*. Back in the 1860s it had been owned by the anarchist Ezra Heywood, and for the second time in the press's long life, the words it printed had gotten its editor in trouble with the law. Judge Chapman had sentenced Fox to two months in jail, which Anderson immediately appealed. Fox was out on $1,000 bond.

Jay Fox at his desk

On the desk rested a small typewriter, the metal casing removed, exposing the gears and springs inside. Fox rolled in a piece of paper, slid the cartridge to the left, and began to write. His hands warmed as letters slamming into the page gained momentum and caught up to the patter of rain outside. "The agitator is the most roundly abused and at the same time most necessary individual in society," Fox typed. "In one generation we hang the agitator and in the next crown his memory with glory."[25]

Words flowed out of him, all that had been welling in him during those days he was forced to listen to the inane arguments of the prosecuting attorney, the spiteful testimony of the deputy sheriff, and finally, the jury's flawed decision. The sentences stacked into paragraphs, the paragraphs crowded onto pages, the pages became storm clouds of words that piled up beside his typewriter and would eventually rain down upon the readers of *The Agitator* in a series titled "The Agitator in History." Fox claimed that *The Tacoma Daily Ledger* had commissioned the piece but refused to publish it because his radical stance didn't "quite suit that subservient capitalist sheet."

"Never in the history of the world was the agitator more in demand than he is today," Fox continued, especially with millions out of work, wealth concentrated among a half dozen billionaires, corruption rampant in politics, and growing slums on the outskirts of every city. "The agitator must come to save the world from its own destruction."[26] Mortal danger awaits a society that suppresses criticism. "Revolution is nothing more than pent-up evolution broke loose," he wrote. "Dam up the river of progress and you will have a tremendous flood on your hands. Let the agitators alone, and they will keep the river clear of obstructions."[27]

Fox defended his position with the United States Constitution. It might seem ironic for an anarchist to cite one of the founding texts of American government, but he argued that the strength of any system is determined by its ability to withstand criticism.

When the American people saw the constitutional convention failed to make provision for the protection of free speech, they realized at once that a most important matter had been overlooked, and set about to remedy the defect. So the first amendment to the Constitution read: "Congress shall make no law abridging the freedom of speech or of the press." This shows us how dearly the people cherished the right of free expression in the early years of this Republic, when the impress of European tyranny was fresh in their minds.[28]

The guarantee of free speech, it seems, might serve as a spillway to relieve the pressure that could topple the whole system, and thus was an essential component to democracy. Fox was not original in pointing this out, but in doing so, he joined a small group of free speech advocates who were putting forth a modern idea of free speech that would be adopted in the century ahead.

✕✕✕

A YEAR LATER, IN FEBRUARY 1913, Fox climbed aboard an eastbound train in Seattle. As the locomotive chugged out of the drizzly lowlands into the foothills of the North Cascades, the conifers were first dusted and then burdened with snow. In the high country, the deep snow berms beside the tracks were a blur, while in the distance the white spires of the encrusted evergreens rotated on the passing slopes, all pointing to the slate-colored crags above. A tunnel in the granite swallowed the train. A howling darkness filled the windows, and when the light returned, it was blinding at first, but everything became more definite as the train journeyed east.

Up ahead, far beyond the horizon, was his destination of Chicago, where *The Agitator* was now being published under a new title, *The Syndicalist.* Over the previous year, even with the help of a defense fund for the trials, Fox had struggled to keep *The Agitator* going. With no advertisements and no other source of revenue than subscriptions and occasional fundraisers, the publication had regularly run a deficit. The only flexible outlay was the meager wages of the editor, and Fox must have felt with growing unease that he couldn't support himself and his family. Following his trial in Tacoma, a brief rally had reduced the deficit to less than twenty dollars, but by October 1912, it ballooned to $51.52, and finally was $77.27 at the time of the second-to-last issue published under the title of *The Agitator.*

William Z. Foster was the one who suggested moving *The Agitator* to Chicago, the hub of industrial America, and changing its name. Foster had stayed with the Foxes in Home during the winter of 1912, taking a respite from hoboing across the United States and lecturing in Wobbly halls. During this visit, Foster converted Fox to his brand of Syndicalism, arguing that it was more effective to "bore from within" established trade unions than to operate outside in radical unions like the Industrial Workers of the World. Given Fox's legal and financial problems, the prospect of relocating the paper and having Foster more directly involved was appealing. "I was impressed by him as by few other labor agitators I have met," Fox wrote of his comrade. "I was struck by his great determination to carry out his plans. He was devoid of that riotous egotism I had found in propagandists. I took to the chap right away and was ready to go along with the program."[29]

Fox and Esther had separated, so he traveled alone. William Z. Foster had something to do with that, as well. Lucy Robins Lang, who lived in Home and knew the trio, wrote: "Jay Fox and Bill Foster resembled each other, though Bill was younger and more sociable. They were about the same height, both slim and lithe, and both imperturbable. Between them moved the dark and voluptuous Esther Fox, a figure of Oriental romance. Later she left Jay for Bill, but the three remained friends."[30] Both men rarely wrote about the details of their personal lives unless it was connected to a larger cause, so how and when the affair started remains unclear. Perhaps during Foster's brief stays in Home, Jay tolerated Esther's longings for their visitor, not knowing that the two would become lifelong companions.

As the train travelled onward, Fox turned from the snow-covered scrub lands of eastern Washington outside his window and read Alexander Berkman's *Prison Memoirs of an Anarchist*, which had just been published by Emma Goldman's Mother Earth Press. He found much that he could identify with in the book. Besides the obvious differences in their circumstances, the two men had a lot in common. Both held anarchist principles that put them at odds with the law. Both had experienced "the pall of silence that descends on a cell house," as Berkman described it; he had spent thirteen years in a Pennsylvania penitentiary for his attempt to assassinate Henry Clay Frick during the 1892 Homestead Strike in Pittsburg. And like Berkman, Fox was inclined to view prison as a brutal manifestation of a capitalist system that cultivates unjust conditions and therefore encourages crime.

After many years in prison, Berkman achieved a measure of maturity as a radical and had compassion for his fellow inmates. While he never abandoned his anarchist principles, nor expressed remorse for the attempted assassination, upon leaving the prison, he devoted himself to exposing the horrid conditions that killed many of his friends there. What had helped him survive the ordeal was the consciousness that he suffered for a great cause. Toward the end of his book Berkman explained: "I looked upon myself as a representative of a world movement; it was my duty to exemplify the spirit and dignity of the ideas it embodied. I was not a prisoner, merely; I was an Anarchist in the hands of the enemy."[31] Fox likely read this toward the end of his journey, somewhere between the undulating grasslands of South Dakota and Minnesota's birch trees.

Perhaps Fox found in Berkman's book a welcome expression of an attitude he needed to sustain himself through his own trial. In November 1912, just before he left, the Washington State Supreme Court had upheld the lower court's decision, and Fox had resolved to appeal his case to the United States Supreme Court.

✗✗✗

THE FREE SPEECH LEAGUE of New York took over the appeals process for Fox's case. Besides donating generously to the defense fund, the organization became actively involved in the case when its secretary Theodore Schroeder wrote a pamphlet titled "The Free Speech Case of Jay Fox," which was distributed nationally. In the pamphlet, Schroeder's argument ran parallel to the one Fox presented in "The Agitator in History," but it was grounded in legal and constitutional analysis. If the "medieval" Washington State law remains on the books, Schroeder wrote, "every reformer of laws will be a criminal and an official 'discretion' will determine who may advocate his reform with impunity. The question is not whether we approve of the opinions of Mr. Fox, but it is rather a question of whether we will help to resist a despotic power that can punish a man for publishing any disapproved opinion."[32]

While Fox waited for a decision on the appeal to the U.S Supreme Court, *The Syndicalist* did not become the weekly he and Foster had envisioned. In September 1913, without notice, it ceased publication. Fox then moved back to Washington State and became vice president of the International Union of Timber Workers in Seattle. There he edited the union's publication *The Timber Worker* and wrote a weekly column, "Letters to Jack Lumber." Almost two years later, still waiting for a decision, Fox settled on a patch of land just across Joe's Bay from Home, where he would remain for the rest of his life.[33]

On February 23, 1915, the Supreme Court reported its decision. In a unanimous opinion written by Oliver Wendell Holmes, the Court upheld the lower court's ruling. "By indirection and unmistakably, the article encouraged and incites a persistence in what we must assume would be a breach of state laws against indecent exposure; and the jury so found," wrote Holmes. "In the present case the disrespect for the law that was encouraged was disregard for it—an overt breach and technically criminal case." Perhaps indicating that he was not entirely comfortable with the Washington State statue in question, but finding no constitutional grounds for overturning it, Holmes concluded: "Of course we have nothing to do with the wisdom of the defendant, the prosecution, or the act. All that concerns us is that it cannot be said to infringe on the Constitution of the United States."[34]

Oliver Wendell Homes was the same Supreme Court Justice who a decade later would compose landmark opinions that articulated a modern conception of free speech based upon the First Amendment. "If there is any principle of the Constitution that more imperatively calls for attachment than any other it is the principle of free thought—not free thought for those who agree with us but freedom for the thought we hate," wrote Holmes in 1929, expressing an idea that could be spliced into one of Jay Fox's or Theodore Schroeder's arguments in favor of free expression.[35]

How could the author of such words have upheld the Fox decision? When Holmes wrote that earlier opinion, the Supreme Court still relied on the bad tendency test for free speech cases. The approach, based upon eighteenth-century English common law, asserted that governments could punish those responsible for publications that have a tendency to cause or incite illegal activity. To recognize the flaws of the bad tendency test, Holmes needed a few more years and the cases of people who ran afoul of laws that severely restricted free speech, such as the Espionage and Seditions Acts passed during World War I. Only then would the arguments of free speech advocates begin to tug on the orbit of his thinking. But the future sets no precedent for the agitator who helps to create it. For now, Fox had to serve his sentence.

)O(O)(

THROUGH THE SPRING and early summer of 1915, Colonel Anderson and an attorney from the timber workers' union named J. G. Brown sought a pardon of Fox's sentence from Washington Governor Ernest C. Lister. In letters, they argued that *The Agitator* had ceased publication and that Fox was now living quietly on a few acres near Home. Although prosecuting attorneys Nolte and Burmeister said they wouldn't object to a pardon, they pointed out several reasons why the governor shouldn't grant one, including the fact that he could not expect a vote from an anarchist like

Fox. Lister refused clemency and ordered Fox to serve at least a portion of his two-month sentence.

On Sunday, July 25, 1915, the people of Home were gathered for their weekly dance in Liberty Hall when they learned of the governor's decision. By then, many of the Prudes had been driven out of the community. Oliver Verity, one of the founders of Home, captured the mood of that time in a letter: "Well, after four years of struggle, the leading prudes have moved away, and I think Home will or has commenced to revive once more." But the reply, written by Roland Muirhead, a Scotsman who had visited Home in the early days, revealed more about how the community had changed: "The gossip you give about various friends who were living in the colony when I had the pleasure of paying a visit is very interesting indeed. I am so sorry, however, that so many have died or gone away."[36] Verity himself was living in Santa Cruz, California, when he wrote his letter, so his view of Home was from a distance.

Few of those in Liberty Hall that summer evening could have foreseen the effect that the absence of all these people would have upon the community. Nor could they sense what hidden, unhealed wounds remained: even with the Prudes gone, the colony had grown accustomed to the factionalism that so often is the first symptom of decline in a utopian experiment. That night, they paused from their dancing to recognize the martyr for their cause and gave three cheers for Jay Fox. All those voices might have been rousing within the confines of Liberty Hall, but outside its walls, the dampened sound rolled down the hill and dispersed across the cold waters of Joe's Bay.

The next day, Deputy Sheriff Fred Shaw arrived from Tacoma and took Fox into custody. A crowd of colonists met the officer and prisoner at the wharf. They shook their comrade's hand and spoke encouraging words. As if to thumb their noses at the proceedings, they informed the sheriff that there was more nude bathing than ever before. "Several people told him that it is still not uncommon to see colonists of either sex enjoying themselves in the water of the bay, clad only in atmospheric robes and sunbeams."[37]

Fox entered the Pierce County Jail, which was located in the basement of the county courthouse building, on Tuesday, July 27, donned a prison uniform, and gave himself over to the routines of prison life. His jailors described him as a model prisoner. Perhaps remembering Berkman's book, he took a compassionate view of his fellow inmates and read aloud to them the works of Ibsen and Tolstoy. Little of the waning summer sunlight penetrated the pile of stone and iron that towered above him.

Fox's attorneys continued to wrangle for a pardon, and on September 11, Governor Lister relented and freed Fox two weeks shy of the full two-month sentence. As Fox left the jail at six o'clock in the evening, the first fresh air he breathed outside was cold and windy. Fox smiled broadly and said nothing to reporters except to express his joy at being released. As he walked away from the courthouse building, a storm was blowing in from the north. Dark clouds soon blotted out the sky and pulsed with lighting, gusts flailed the tree branches, pellets of hail collected on the grass, torrential rains sluiced down the streets. It was not recorded where Fox waited out this strange weather, but soon his friends would celebrate his return to Home.

Life at Home: Education

"THE MIND OF THE TEACHER must direct in the school room, but in that, as well as in national affairs, that government is best which governs the least," asserted George Allen, both a parent and school teacher, in the pages of *Discontent.* "What kind of fruit will it bring forth? I do not know, but I am convinced that better and more natural boys and girls will be the product than those that have been cramped by coercive and, for the most part, foolish restrictions of our common schools." Rather than relying upon an educational approach that promoted capitalism and forced conformity, he advocated the use of reason. "The only just method is to present all known ideas and then appeal to the pupils to judge for themselves as to what is right. If this method were followed the latent love of justice would develop in them and not be smothered by the forced growth of patriotism and hero worship."[1]

Whether this philosophy was practiced in Home's schoolroom depended largely upon the aptitude of the teacher. In the early days, Alice Kelley taught in the one-room schoolhouse near the water. Traveling Scotsman Roland Muirhead met her on his 1901 visit and described her as a woman of average height, in her forties, with red hair and dark eyes and complexion. He thought she looked "to be a very exceptional and high-minded woman." She seems to have embodied Allen's philosophy: "If scholars won't behave, blames herself and says must be something amiss about with herself. Searches herself accordingly."[2] Of her forty dollars a month salary, she retained for herself twenty-five, saving the rest for the construction of a new schoolhouse.

It is likely Kelley in an undated photograph of fifteen schoolchildren squinting in the bright sunlight. They cluster on the exposed hillside, girls in dark dresses, boys in overalls, school teacher gazing toward the water. A single child smiles, the girl with pigtails down in the lower right. This image has the same impenetrable quality as the other photographs of the school in Home: rows of pupils convey little information about the school itself, and the group occupies too much foreground to provide context. All it offers are faces, but the names they all knew so well are now forgotten, even to those

Schoolchildren of
Home

who grew up in Home. A note accompanying the photograph reads, "Mr. Dadisman could identify none of these."[3]

After the original schoolhouse burned in 1903, classes moved to a room on the ground floor of Liberty Hall, right next to the printing office. For a few years, James F. Morton, Jr., led the school, and perhaps the proximity to *The Demonstrator*, his first and true passion, contributed to his poor performance as teacher. The children did not listen to his lectures with the same polite attentiveness as adults. It was enough to make him lose his patience. A critic of Home's school likely had Morton in mind when he wrote: "Another comrade, who is one of our best declaimers on the right of free speech, has been known to command the children in his care to 'shut up' and to enforce commands by superior strength."[4]

Visitors to Home often noted that the children did not share the values of their parents. In 1907, one commented in *The Demonstrator* that the children showed little inclination toward radicalism and loved baseball and dancing far too much. He recommended dedicating an evening each month to entertainments with a radical bent: "heart-to-heart talks, concerts, stereopticon views of the French revolution, the Civil War, and the great class struggles of the world, bringing before them the great thinkers, the champions of liberty, the martyrs who died for a better future for the race."[5]

In 1911, the school moved to a handsome schoolhouse on top of the hill. "The plan of light inlet is in accordance with the best ideas, coming from one side only, and flowing over the shoulders of the pupils," announced *The Agitator* in praise of its design. "The workmanship is good; and the architectural outlines very pleasing to the sense of beauty."[6] In spite of this quality, at least one visitor, J. C. Harrison, complained that the curriculum taught in this particular building was too conventional: "The school sports 'Old Glory' and the children are taught that George Washington never told a lie."[7]

Yet a boy who attended this school, Eugene Travaglio, would remember it at the age of ninety in utopian terms:

> In simple language, political myths were dissipated, economic panaceas riddled with holes, and the validity of bogus moral issues questioned, to the utter dismay of State School Inspectors sent there to ascertain to what level of depravity the children had been subjected to by their teachers, and to what extent the children had been exposed to the radicalism of their elders. But, let this be said, truancy from this school was unknown.[8]

Other children from Home had different sorts of memories. One recalled the time that George Cowell and Ed Halperin snuck a dead skunk into the stove. Radium LaVene shot spit balls at a teacher named Frederick Noah, who in turn chucked erasers at his pupils. When the school board held a meeting, Mr. Noah admitted that he could not control the children and was asked to resign. Radium, listening to proceedings through the ventilation shaft under the school, felt like a first class heel.[9]

CHAPTER FIVE
How Cain Dies in the Twentieth Century

AS HE WALKED THE SODDEN PLANKS of the Municipal Dock, his eyes wandered from overcoats to leather shoes, across roped bollards to steam rising off the mills. He sighed a lungful of cigarette smoke. Tacoma's dreary, wet weather could not compare to the glorious blue skies of Los Angeles. Drizzle saturated everything here, but in California the wind rustling the palms reminded a man of the nearby ocean, even when the views were framed in hotel and automobile windows, or caught in the short walks to and from a courthouse. It felt good to be alone though, not shadowed by a bodyguard: protection is another word for confinement. Soon enough, he would be on the familiar slope above Joe's Bay and tucked into his mother's cabin.

Donald Vose may have looked like a well-heeled sport, in a dark suit and tie, with his hair trim on the sides and parted on top, but the bags beneath his eyes betrayed the things that he had witnessed. There were the late nights drinking cheap whiskey with anarchists and dynamiters. The agony of sitting on hard seats in cramped courtrooms that didn't permit smoking. Matthew A. Schmidt upon the stand jabbing a thick finger in his direction and accusing him, the star witness, of lying. "Let me ask you, gentlemen, do you believe Donald Vose?" Schmidty had asked the jury, his German accent putting a hard edge on his words. "You would not whip your dog on the testimony of a creature like Vose. No honest man would. Any man who would believe Vose would not deserve to have a dog."[1] Well, Schmidty got life in prison, so no need to worry about seeing him again.

Approaching the steamer to Home, he encountered a group of men who had just arrived from that place. The year before, the guys would have smiled at his familiar face, perhaps teased him for his fancy suit and tie, but on this day, January 26, 1916, they beset him in "a murderous attack," "a bitter fight," according to the newspapers.[2] Fists collided with flesh. A cigarette tumbled and fizzed against the damp boards. Vose fled the barrage and leapt aboard the steamer to Seattle, the one he had just debarked. The officers on the ship refused to let his attackers onboard.

They stood just beyond the rails, probably hurling the invectives with which he would be branded for the rest of his life: *Rat! Stool pigeon! Cur! Traitor! Liar! Judas Iscariot!*

Vose retreated further onto the boat, which took him back to Seattle, back to the office of the Burns Detective Agency, back to the safety of bodyguards and undisclosed locations.

✕✕✕

IN THE 1910S AND 1920S, the children raised in Home began to come of age, but they seemed uninterested in staying in the colony or taking over the anarchist experiment. The parents had taken a non-coercive approach to childrearing. One parent expressed their philosophy this way: "How far into freedom are we willing to take them with us? Shall we leave them in their present status and go on, or shall we turn and reach out hands in fellowship, leading ever along our journey, wherever that may take us, as far as they may wish to go our way? If they outstrip us, well and good."[3] Out of principle, the parents would not force their children to be anything but themselves.

The children carried into adulthood memories of enjoying unconventional freedoms, running down to the dock to greet the daily steamer, playing Fox and Geese on the beach, throwing their naked bodies into sun-warmed tidewater, digging clams and eating them in the light of bonfires, attending community dances, joining in the choruses of Wobbly songs, and sliding down the snow-slick hill above Joe's Bay.[4] They would also remember the constant ferment of ideas, the heated discussions about the issues of the day, the well-stocked libraries, the atmosphere that encouraged questioning and challenging authority. For the children of Home, utopia lay somewhere in their yesterdays, not in their tomorrows. Their exposure to an anarchist way of life encouraged an independence of spirit and open-mindedness that would lead them, if not to the radicalism of their parents, then on to successful lives.

All four Allen daughters went on to earn college degrees in a time when few women did so. Ellen Falk graduated from Stadium High School in Tacoma at the age of fifteen. Her younger brother Ernie entered the University of Washington at the age of fourteen, reputedly the youngest to have ever enrolled there; he applied his intellect to the study of law and received a law degree at the age of twenty-one. Rose Ostroff Payne made it into *Who's Who in America* and the pages of *Time* magazine for her contributions to hematology. As a research scientist at Stanford, she studied the antibodies that form during blood transfusions and advanced the understanding of why bodies reject organ transplants. Virna Haffer, the daughter of the man who expressed Home's parenting philosophy, became a renowned photographer and expert in photograms. She was one of the first people to create images by placing swamp grass, twigs, grasshopper wings, metal shavings, fish bones, and other materials onto photographic paper and then exposing it to light. Her work was exhibited nationally and abroad. Radium LaVene, who was named after the recently discovered element, established himself as a successful businessman in California. Later in life, he gathered stories and reminiscences of his birthplace in an unpublished manuscript titled "There Was No Place like Home."[5]

Yet among the children of Home, Donald Vose stood out. None rejected their parents' ideals as completely and defiantly as he did, and in his hapless rebellion, he achieved a kind of immortality.

)O(O(

BY 1910, DONALD VOSE WAS EIGHTEEN, too old to play with the kids on the wharf or the beach, but not going anywhere in particular either. He picked up odd jobs in Home and drifted up and down the coast, showing up on the doorsteps of his mother's anarchist friends, staying with them for a while, then moving on. When people remembered him, they described him as a sullen, lazy, aimless youth, inept and bumbling at whatever he did.[6] Yet it seems every description of him is tainted by who he became and what he did.

Who knows what Vose actually thought of what was called "The Crime of the Century"? In the early hours of October 10, 1910, an infernal device—an alarm clock connected with wires to sticks of dynamite—ticked away against a wall of the *Los Angeles Times* building. Upstairs close to a hundred people were working, putting the next day's edition to bed. The bomb detonated at 1:07 a.m., shearing off a wall of stone and brick. A series of explosions followed, tearing through the structure and igniting the ink barrels in the alley. It was as if the building had been made to incinerate: gas from the heat pipes, wooden floorboards, and rolls of newspaper all fed the flames. People leapt and scrambled for their lives. By sunrise, the burned and injured filled the hospitals, and twenty were dead. On the street, crowds watched smoke billowing out of the ruins. To one side of the building, an ugly hole was fringed with bent girders and rubble. A substantial chunk of the stone edifice remained standing, the interior within gutted and charred. On the roof, a bronze eagle still perched, its wings arched as if ready to take flight. At a glance, the dark silhouette resembled a prehistoric raptor trying to escape the chaos below.

The newspaper's owner, General Harrison Gray Otis, had erected the eagle as an emblem of the industrial freedom he openly advocated in the pages of his newspaper. The bombing only delayed the paper briefly, and from an auxiliary location nearby, the *Times* declared on its front page: "Unionist Bombs Wreck the Times; Many Seriously Injured." There was no evidence for blaming the unions other than the fact that Los Angeles was embroiled in a fierce battle between business owners and labor unions. Otis and his allies in the Merchants and Manufacturers Association stridently promoted Los Angeles as an "open shop" town, advocating for the ability to hire non-union and union workers alike. In practice this meant that wages were lower in Los Angeles than elsewhere in California, and that summer, labor leaders from San Francisco had poured into town, attempting to organize labor and "equalize" wages. There were numerous strikes, and in response the *Times* vociferously attacked the union leaders. Los Angeles began to feel like a war zone between unions and industrialists. Otis mounted a small cannon on the hood of his limousine, and it seemed only a matter of time before his paper would become a target.

By the time Donald Vose got involved, nobody was calling it "The Crime of the Century" any more. The law-and-order element had already confirmed for themselves that "there still was a God in Israel": the McNamara brothers, having confessed to the crime, were locked up in San Quentin. James J. McNamara, who took the blame for acquiring and planting the bomb in the *Times* bombing, got a life sentence. His brother John B., formerly the secretary-treasurer of the International Association of Bridge and Structural Iron Workers, was serving a fifteen-year sentence.[7] Yet as the twentieth century ticked away, barreling onward to other crimes that would mock the hyperbolic moniker, certain culprits involved in this crime remained at large. William J. Burns, the detective who apprehended the McNamaras, had to conclude his memoir of the investigation, published in 1913, with this embarrassing admission: "Of the two Anarchists, Schmidt and Caplan, supplied to help J. B. McNamara in the destruction of the Times Building, all that can be said is that they are yet to be captured and to be made to answer to the charge of murder."[8]

No one knows for sure how Donald Vose became an informant for Burns. The Burns operatives who tramped around Home in 1910 in the guise of surveyors did stay at his sister's place. Some claimed that these same operatives intervened when Vose was caught in an act of petty thievery and used the event to blackmail him into their services.[9] A more likely scenario, however, is that Vose was broke and had too much time on his hands. Perhaps he even nurtured a pipe dream of collecting the rewards for Schmidt and Caplan. The total amount of $10,000 was nearly sixteen times what the average working stiff could earn in a year. But Vose, who never liked working hard, probably found that he didn't have the capital to undertake the search. He needed some backing.

By his account, in September 1913, he knocked on the door of the Seattle office of the Burns Detective Agency. He said he was from Home and had grown up among the anarchists. Maybe he even dropped hints that his mother was friends with Emma Goldman. Soon he was talking to Manager Walter R. Thayer, offering his services. "Do you still want to catch Caplan and Schmidt?" he asked.

"You bet we do," Thayer said.

"I can help you get both of them."[10]

)O)O(

I sit at a large wooden table in the Key Peninsula Historical Society Museum. It has a pleasant, musty smell, and in the windowless room around me are yellowing photographs of the local baseball teams, old bottles made of thick and chipped glass, treadle sewing machines, and other assorted artifacts. Jay Fox's old hand press stands against one wall. Between its plates rest, somewhat anachronistically, photocopies of *Discontent*, which visitors can take with them. Several binders of material on Home sprawl before me, and I flip through them, examining the documents and photographs. I'm not really looking for Donald Vose, but he waits for me there like a specter.

I've read about him in various places, and questions nag at the facts of his story: Who was this young man before he became the reviled stool pigeon? What actually motivated him to do what he did? Did he consciously reject the values of his parents or did his actions originate in an unconscious drive that propelled him into a situation that he lost control of? At what point did he understand that his actions would destroy his relationship with everything and everyone he had known? Did he even care?

Most of the information about Vose's youth, of the time before he became a villain, a black sheep among the anarchists, a young man sent wandering like Cain, is invariably biased. What few glimpses there are come from his own mother, Gertrude Vose, who wanted to raise him to be a rebellious little anarchist. "I have a young boy about as impetuous as they make 'em," she bragged in a letter to a friend in 1901, when he was nine years old. "No child likes to be forced, and it certainly destroys the noble impulses and nourishes objectionable characteristics. He says he won't sing God and patriotic songs in school, and told the teacher he didn't want to carry the flag; but she had him do it just the same."[11]

Gertie Vose wrote this just before she brought her son to Home. A single mother who had long ago separated from the boy's father, she moved to Joe's Bay in part to find a suitable place to raise her son. Once settled there, Gertie Vose thrived in a community of like-minded people but struggled financially like many other colonists. She occasionally had to take work away from the colony for months at time, hiring herself out as a domestic in Tacoma. Young Donald Vose was left in the care of relatives who had followed his mother to Home. As he grew into adolescence, references to the boy appear in *The Demonstrator*, his name listed among residents out picking hops or picnicking on the beach, but these notes offer little evidence to explain the sullen disposition so many people later described.

Yet for all I know about Donald Vose, all that I've read about him, I've never seen him. Then I turn the page in one of the binders, and there he is staring out at me from a photograph of three young men. The handwritten names below the photograph—Richie Bowles, Frank Pease, Donald Vose—identify him as the last one in the lineup, on the right, leaning against the rail. The young men, perhaps in their late teens or early twenties, pose with unlit cigarettes, trying to look like sports. Richie Bowles and Frank Pease wear scarves, as if dressed like cowboys, while Donald Vose is decked out in an overcoat, suit, and tie. The hat on his head seems precariously balanced upon his hair. What is the occasion they're dressed for? Are those flecks of rain on Vose's jacket or smudges on the photograph?

Three young men of Home

I lean toward the image, then away. His eyes follow me. I examine his face, the round and jowly chin, the pursed lips, the eyes that seem guilty and wounded at the same time. His demeanor possesses a certain vulnerability not present in the other boys' faces. I cannot stare too long into Vose's eyes; behind their dullness lingers an accusation, a petition, an anguish. But maybe he's just hoodwinking me too, maybe I'm seeing more than what's there, and maybe that's what caused people to trust him.

)O)O(

DONALD SITS IN THE SALOON, a squalid dump that sells rotgut whiskey for a nickel, speaking to the man he believes can save him. Darkness fills the grimy windows. A few lamps throw illuminated circles on the dingy walls then fade into a languid glow, creating the impression that the scene is taking place at the bottom of the ocean. Donald's gut is knotted, and he wants to confess the reason for his betrayal.

His feet kicking uneasily through the sawdust on the floor, he blurts out: "I couldn't go on believing forever that the gang was going to change the world by shooting off their loud traps on soap boxes and sneaking around blowing up a lousy building or a bridge! I got wise it was all a crazy pipe dream."[12]

)O)O(

IT DIDN'T TAKE LONG to find the first fugitive. Donald Vose only had to ask around Home and soon enough he was in the small town of Rolling Bay on Bainbridge Island, just across the water from Seattle. Vose later claimed that he had waited outside the barbershop until everyone left, then entered and climbed into the chair. The barber didn't recognize him, just did his job: draped the gown around him, snapped it behind his neck, lathered his face, sharpened the razor on the strop, and then began scraping the blade down his cheeks. The barber had aged, his hair gone gray, his large brown eyes glazed and distracted. Yet Donald Vose recognized him. "You are David Caplan, aren't you?" he said, his face half-covered with soap.

Caplan stood there dumbstruck. His eyes, suddenly focused, flitted uncertainly. Should he attack or run?

But then the young man in the chair reassured him. He said that he was Donald, Gertie Vose's son, and that he had come from Home to warn him that he had been seen entering the settlement. People were talking.

Caplan was so relieved that he invited the youth back to his shack in the woods. They walked through the damp, January darkness, two miles over slippery mud to a small tract where he was raising chickens. The two stayed up late into the night talking. While on the lam for the previous three and a half years, Caplan had not been able to see his wife and children or many of his comrades, and the loneliness was torturing him. He described how he had to work himself ragged, keeping himself busy day and night, just to avoid doing something rash. The next day, as Donald Vose was leaving, Caplan told him to return whenever he had time.

And he did come back. He visited several times, staying for extended periods in the winter and early spring of 1914, listening to Caplan speak about his peregrinations since the bombing. From a farm in Cle Elum, Washington, to London, England, then Johannesburg, South Africa, and on to France, Italy, Germany, and Belgium, then back through North America, to Quebec, New York City, and Detroit. A comrade had given him funds to buy the chicken farm on Bainbridge Island. Caplan also confided that he was trying to get in touch with Schmidty, the other suspect in the case. Vose offered to help: maybe he could carry a letter.[13]

✗◯✗◯✗

EMMA GOLDMAN WAS IN LOS ANGELES when she received word that Donald Vose had appeared on the doorstep of the *Mother Earth* headquarters in New York City. The publication, housed in a four-story brownstone at 74 West 119th Street, was a nexus for radicals and anarchists. The boy had presented a letter from his mother to Alexander Berkman, Goldman's co-editor at *Mother Earth*. Gertie Vose had been one of the few who staunchly supported Berkman during his long prison confinement, and her child knew no one in the city, so how could they turn him away? Berkman gave him a room on the second floor, above the office and printing shop, and just beneath Goldman's own apartment.

Goldman was in the midst of a busy West Coast tour, so this information probably quickly faded into the background. She had other pressing concerns, chief among them the war breaking out in Europe and the increasing militarism in the United States. She did, however, travel up the coast and pay a visit to Donald Vose's mother. The two had not seen each other in sixteen years. They had first met in 1898, when Goldman was rising to prominence on an early West Coast speaking tour. At the time, Gertie Vose was living in Scio, Oregon, with a new lover. Goldman had read some of Gertie Vose's contributions to such publications as *The Firebrand* and gladly accepted the invitation to stay in Scio. They corresponded for a while afterward, but the letters dropped off as the whirlwind of Goldman's life gained momentum and Vose settled into her life in Home.

It was a pleasant but ultimately disappointing reunion in Home. "We talked of the old days and old friends," Goldman later wrote. "I learned how cruelly hard life had been with Gertie; how it had whipped her body, but her spirit was the same, though more mellowed by disappointment, by pain and sorrow. Her one great joy, however, was that her boy had finally gotten into the right atmosphere, that now he would become a man active in the movement. She told me of the glowing reports he was writing about Berk (as he called Berkman), the unemployed and antimilitary activities in New York at the time, and how interested Donald had become."[14]

When Goldman returned to New York on September 15, 1914, the affairs of *Mother Earth* absorbed her attention, so much so that at first she forgot about the uninvited guest. Facing bankruptcy, she could no longer afford the large brownstone and had to find another location for the publication. All of the inhabitants, including herself, had to move out too. She then remembered Donald Vose. "I reproached myself for such neglect of him," she later wrote. She knocked on his door. "My first impression of Donald Vose was not agreeable; perhaps because of his high-pitched, thin voice and shifting eyes. But he was Gertie's son, out of work, wretchedly clad, unhealthy in appearance. I stifled my aversion and told him that as I was about to give up the house, he might go to the little farm on the Hudson belonging to a friend of ours."

He listened to her, his eyes perpetually drifting away from hers and glancing from the walls and corners of the little room to the floor littered with cigarette butts and discarded clothes. When she finished, he told her that he was already planning to return to the West. He had lost his job as a chauffeur and was waiting for money. "The main thing, however, delaying his departure from New York, Donald said, was the message given to him by someone in Washington for M. A. Schmidt, the delivery of which was imperative."

〉〈〉〈

MOST OF SEPTEMBER 26, 1914, Donald Vose spent knocking around town with Terry Carlin, whom he knew from San Francisco. Just back from London, Carlin regaled Vose with tales of life overseas. As they leaned their elbows on the rough-cut tabletops of a saloon and chatted away in the shadows, Vose surely footed the bill for the countless rounds of drinks. Pulling in as much as five dollars a day from the Burns Detective Agency, he could blow it on cheap whiskey and beer for himself and his friends.

Carlin was a charismatic sponger who hung around radical circles. Although in sympathy with anarchism, he was less attracted to agitation and more inclined to a life of enlightened dissipation. He once wrote to a friend, encapsulating his philosophy: "I am very 'crummy,' badly flea-bitten, overrun with bed bugs, somewhat flyblown, but redemption of it all, I am free and always drunk."[15] After he quit working, he seems to have subsisted entirely on his charm and the good graces of others. Many who knew him, including Jack London, Theodore Dreiser, and Eugene O'Neill, admired him and were drawn to his brilliant conversations.

As Donald Vose glanced from the ever-chatting mouth in Carlin's gaunt face to the bristles on his unshaven chin, to the stained and open collar of his flannel shirt, to his long fingers searching and scratching at the lice in his battered and threadbare suit, the younger man perhaps saw in Carlin a father figure, a role model. While under the spell of this raconteur, while the wash of his words rolled over him, maybe Vose even forgot his mission. He could dream of one day being free and always drunk too, but inevitably the tab always came, reminding him of the source of all his cash.

Vose had spent the entire summer waiting and trying to locate M. A. Schmidt. With the man was in hiding, the letter remained undelivered. Now, the jaundiced light of autumn was filtering into the city, and he was no closer to finding Schmidty. And that Goldman woman had just told him he must move out along with everyone else, but as Carlin spoke, he could sip and almost ignore his problems.

They picked up a bottle of whiskey on their way back to West 119th Street, climbed the stoop, and entered the house. There is some dispute among the witnesses about what happened next. According to Emma Goldman, a few friends meeting with M. A. Schmidt upstairs heard Carlin and Vose stumbling back to his room. A letter was mentioned, and the boy was called to Goldman's room. The meeting lasted no more than ten minutes, the conversation was general, the letter was delivered.[16]

Donald Vose's version is more sensational and detailed. He sat in his room, drinking with Terry Carlin. Two writers, Hutchins Hapgood and Lincoln Steffens, stood there listening to Carlin speak of his trip to London. Then Alexander Berkman descended the stairs and pulled Vose aside, telling him he had gotten a telegram that Schmidty was in town; the wanted man would visit the house this evening. Perhaps under the pretense of getting more whiskey, Vose ducked out to contact a Burns operative. When Vose returned, he and Carlin resumed drinking in his room. The door was open, and a man passed on the stairs.

"I guess that's Schmidty," Carlin said.[17]

They followed him up to Emma Goldman's room, and there sat a group of four or five people. "Meet a friend of ours," Berkman said, introducing Donald Vose to M. A. Schmidt. Vose took in Schmidty's physical characteristics: wavy hair, ruddy cheeks, stubby blond moustache, six feet tall, powerfully built physique beneath a fine suit. When they shook hands, Schmidty's viselike grip could have crushed Donald's thin knuckles.

Vose later claimed that Schmidty told him all kinds of things at this meeting. That Schmidty was going by the alias Joe Hoffman. That he'd had a hell of a time staying clear of the police for the past four years. That he'd destroyed the laundry marks on his clothing to avoid identification. As they talked, their eyes could not meet, not just because of Donald's traveling gaze but because Schmidty had only one eye. Schmidty had bought a new glass eye for himself on Fifth Avenue, as unlike his old one as possible. Donald would later tell reporters: "He had always asked strangers walking on his left side to exchange sides with him on account of his left side blindness, arguing that no one would believe that a guilty man would himself call attention to one of the surest badges of his identity."[18]

✕✕✕

ONCE THE LETTER WAS DELIVERED to Schmidty, Vose continued knocking around New York, drinking with Terry Carlin and others. Maybe they ended up at the Irish saloon euphemistically called the Golden Swan—or the Hell Hole, as it was more commonly known—that would become one of Carlin's haunts. Here, gangsters, gamblers, teamsters, truckers, tarts, pimps, and whores crowded around the wooden tables. Artists and writers frequented the place too. In 1917 John Sloan would make an etching of its interior, the drunken cackles inside the room nearly spilling out of the wild lines of image. Eugene O'Neill, who looks out of the upper-right side of the etching, would later set one of his most famous plays, *The Iceman Cometh*, in a saloon modeled on the Hell Hole. Donald Vose could be sitting somewhere just beyond the border of the drawing, stooped forward, listening to Terry Carlin.

The din of conversation and laughter saturated the room, which now and again was drowned out by the rattling approach and roaring rumble of the elevated train passing on the tracks just outside. Maybe Vose even blew his Burns pay on an evening or two with one of the tarts he saw flirting and throwing legs upon the men around him. The city devoured his bank

"Hell Hole" by
John Sloan

rolls, consumed day and night in a blur beyond the grimy windows. He could have learned from Carlin how to subsist on free lunch counters and cheap bags of oysters from Fulton Market, but there were times in the day when the saloons closed and emptied out.[19] Vose would then drift over to the office of *Mother Earth* to warm up. Emma Goldman remembered him sitting there, loafing on a bench day after day, his clothes becoming shabbier and shabbier. He had no overcoat, but rumors circulated about him having no shortage of cash for carousing.

Schmidty was among the folks Vose and Carlin drank with. If Vose's story is to be believed, Schmidty practically confessed his involvement in the bombing of the *Los Angeles Times* building over drinks at the Woodstock Hotel. Speaking with a thick German accent, Schmidty said that General Otis and his paper were enemies of organized labor, that the bombing had not achieved its goal because Otis was yet alive, that they had only succeeded in snuffing out twenty lives. Schmidty admitted that he wished that he'd done the job alone: "He could have avoided detection and covered up his tracks, too many people in San Francisco knew of their plan and that whole thing was a blunder and bunglingly done from the beginning to end."[20] One of the guys who had helped in the plot, Eric Morton, had gotten drunk and lost the key to the apartment where they had stashed some of the dynamite. Too afraid to ask for a new key, Morton abandoned the dynamite, and as a result, Burns later found it and traced it back to the company where they had bought it. As the men leaned in close, whispering their secrets and swilling away drinks on Burns's dime, surely a detective or two lingered outside, waiting to trail the suspect back to his hideout.

As this shivering derelict of a boy kept washing up like jetsam into the office of *Mother Earth*, as more and more people reported of his treating companions to round after round, Emma Goldman became annoyed at his presence. One day she asked him why he didn't buy warm clothes for himself. He told little lies about waiting for a fare to return to Washington, then later lied again and told her that the fare had come and he'd spent it all. His constant flow of cash became suspicious. Goldman discreetly inquired through her contacts in Washington whether anyone was sending him money. When she learned no one was, she became even more apprehensive of his presence. It was not uncommon for paid spies, agents of the enemy, to infiltrate radical groups.

Then Vose came to her, said his fare had finally arrived. A week later he left town, and she reproached herself for thinking badly of Gertie Vose's son. Soon afterward, both Schmidty and Caplan were arrested.

✕✕✕

"I'LL ADMIT WHAT I TOLD YOU last night was a lie—that bunk about getting patriotic and my duty to my country. But here's the real reason," Donald says, sitting in the saloon. No matter how much he squirms, he can't shake this awful feeling. And it gets his goat how the man across from him doesn't seem to give a damn what happens to him. It's like being a half-drugged, half-dead bug stuck through with a pin in a display case, and the only thing that he can do with this infuriating agony is spill his guts: "The only reason! It was just for the money! I got stuck on a whore and wanted dough to blow in on her and have a good time! That's all I did it for! Just money! Honest."

The man across from Donald grabs his labels and shakes him. "God damn you, shut up!" he says. "What the hell is it to me?"[21]

✕✕✕

TOY WAS BARKING on the front porch. Strange men provoked in her a high-pitched, ragged *yap! yap!* that grew in ferocity the closer they came. Lucy Robins Lang hoped whoever it was would just keep walking. She had just returned with her husband Bob Robins to San Francisco, and many of her radical friends were gloomy. The city itself had slumped into an economic depression, the labor movement had declined since the McNamara trial, and now Caplan and Schmidt were in custody. Schmidty they had apprehended on a street corner in New York City, and Caplan they caught in his shack in the middle of the night. At both arrests, a Burns detective was present among the police officers, which raised the suspicion that an insider had tipped them off. As bad as this news was, it was dwarfed by the war raging in Europe. Many radicals had expected the proletariat to rise up against the imperialists, but now workers and poor people were killing each other in the trenches. Toy's howling increased, tugging Lang out of her thoughts. Someone knocked.

Lucy Robins Lang opened the door, and there stood a tall, gangly boy she had not seen in four years. "My mother sent me to you," he said. "I'm from Home Colony—Gertrude Vose's son, Donald. Remember me?" He lit a cigarette, inhaled, fished a letter out of his pocket, and gave it to her.

"Where is your mother?" Lang asked, taking the letter.

"In the colony," he replied, his words filled with smoke. "She'll never leave that place."

They had to raise their voices above Toy's incessant barking. The little hound angrily snuffled his pant cuffs and then nipped at his ankle. Vose cursed and Lang ordered the dog to stop. Tail between her legs, Toy plodded back to her corner of the porch and lay down.

"I'm expecting a job in a couple days and I haven't got a room."

Lang didn't like the boy, but out of fondness for Gertie Vose, she agreed to let him stay in one of their many rooms. A few days after he installed himself in their home, Lang received word that some old friends were coming to town. It was as good an excuse as any to ask Vose to leave. She went upstairs and knocked on the door. No one answered, so she pushed it open and frowned at what she saw: the contents of two suitcases strewn about the room and cigarette butts and matches discarded on the floor. In his stuff, she saw leaflets for a talk given by Emma Goldman and Alexander Berkman in New York City. Why would Vose by carrying these? She reached for them, and her hand brushed against something cold and steel. She immediately rushed downstairs and found her husband.

"Donald has a gun!" she told him. "He's a spy!"

Bob Robins calmed her down, not wanting to jump to conclusions, and convinced her to get help from Eric Morton, a friend and fellow anarchist. The next afternoon, while Donald Vose was out again, Lang and Morton combed through his belongings. They found two revolvers, a cartridge belt, notebooks filled with names and addresses, and messages written in a bizarre code. Morton, schooled in Burns espionage jargon, deciphered the notes and pieced together Vose's trail from Home to Bainbridge Island to New York to this house in San Francisco. They learned that Burns planned to keep Donald Vose in hiding with Lang until the trial, so that he would seem like just another comrade on the witness stand.

Lang wanted Vose out of her house immediately, but Morton convinced her to let him stay so they could conduct a little bit of counterespionage on Burns. They planned to shadow Vose and determine the machinations of the hated detective. Driving lessons were the ruse. Lang and her husband owned a car, and Vose loved to drive, especially if it was fast, so she pretended she wanted him to teach her. As they motored through San Francisco with Eric Morton and his comrades following close behind, Lang tried to see whether the Judas in their midst had any virtues whatsoever: "Except for a certain feeling for his mother, he had none. He had not the least sense of right or wrong and only the most rudimentary intelligence." Lang and her friends briefly entertained the idea of kidnapping the boy on one of these driving trips and holding him for ransom, but Schmidty, who knew of these plans from his jail cell, dissuaded them. It might mean a hanging for him and Caplan.

In order to keep up the subterfuge, Lang and her friends didn't tell the wider community of radicals about Vose's treachery. Rumors began to circulate that Vose would testify in the case, but no one yet knew for certain that he was an informant. Lang was incensed to hear that people thought she was shielding him, and she had to set things straight. When she told the truth to Alexander Berkman, who had come from New York to organize Schmidty's defense, he wanted to kill the boy, and it took everything she had to restrain him.

Vose stayed with Lang and her husband until just before the trial and then left of his own accord. They watched the stool pigeon walk down the street, with who knows how many men trailing behind him. Toy barked herself delirious at the window.[22]

)X(X()X(

AS THE STATE'S PRINCIPAL WITNESS, Donald Vose had a story that could destroy the lives of two men, and to tell it, his own life began to resemble those of the fugitives he helped catch. The big difference, however, was that he was now openly on the side of people he had been raised to see as the enemy. Hiding in secret, he now relied on them for safety and sustenance.

Still, he had numerous brushes with the animosity and open violence that he would encounter again and again. In the lobby of the Stowell Hotel in Los Angeles, two known anarchists approached and asked him to join them for a drink. They had a car waiting outside. Vose refused. He had just arrived and was on his way to speak with investigators for the trial. The anarchists had hoped to abduct Vose, but when they realized he would not come peaceably, one of the men rushed at him and threatened: "We'll get you; you had no business deserting us!" Seeing that the altercation might come to blows, Vose's bodyguard, a former prizefighter, knocked the man to the floor. Both anarchists scrambled out of the lobby and took off in the car.[23]

On the stand, Donald Vose delivered the payload of his incriminating evidence. He spoke of meeting Schmidty at Emma Goldman's and at the

Woodstock Hotel. Surely coached by Burns and the district attorney, he portrayed Schmidty as a conspirator in a plot to murder and destroy with dynamite, a killer who showed no remorse and even regretted that more people had not died. Toward the end of his testimony, he described growing up among anarchists and how he became an informant for Burns.

"Do you expect to go back to Home Colony to live?" the district attorney asked.

"No, not after this," the witness said. "It would not be healthy for me to go there."[24]

And if Vose had any doubts about how he would be received, the defense trundled out people who knew him in Home in an attempt to discredit him. Both residents and frequent visitors spoke of their low opinion of the witness's character and even mentioned that he was once caught stealing money, but because they could be written off as denizens of an anarchist colony themselves, their testimony did not have the desired effect. "The situation was little less than ludicrous," the *Los Angeles Times* commented.[25]

The most damning attack came from Schmidty himself. Although Schmidty admitted to using dynamite to retaliate against the harsh tactics of the industrialists, he denied any involvement in the bombing of the *Los Angeles Times* building. And when it came to the subject of his accuser, he asked the jury: "Let me ask you, gentlemen, do you believe Donald Vose? You would not whip your dog on the testimony of a creature like Vose. No honest man would. Any man who would believe Vose would not deserve to have a dog." The jury believed Vose enough to convict Schmidty of the crime and commit him to life in prison.

ⅩⅪⅨ

EMMA GOLDMAN SEETHED WITH RAGE at the perfidy of Vose. "It was the most terrible blow of my public life in twenty-five years," she would write. This was a significant statement coming from someone who had been arrested and locked up by the police, demonized, hounded, libeled by newspapers, and labeled "the high priestess of anarchism" and "the most dangerous woman in America." She could shrug off the ignorance and greed of her closed-minded contemporaries, but this time the assault had come from within, from a child of the movement, a boy who had been reared in the atmosphere of liberty. On top of that, she'd had to swallow her disgust at that untidy, ungrateful cur, and he returned the favor by betraying the cause.

Goldman wanted to expose the spy and release the magma of hatred swelling inside her, but the attorneys working with Schmidty asked her to wait, to keep quiet until the trial was over. They didn't want her words to sway the trial either way, but with Schmidty locked up for life, what difference did it make now? She published the article "Donald Vose, the Accursed" in the January 1916 issue of *Mother Earth.*

The article recounted events from her perspective, mingled with traces of her own emotional turmoil. She was writing primarily to the radical groups that Vose lived among, which were then circulating rumors that an informant had helped to catch Schmidt and Caplan. The imagery consistently drew a connection between Judas Iscariot and Donald Vose. Both broke bread with and befriended men whom they betrayed into the meshes of a partial and cruel justice. But at the end of the article, her rhetoric became Old Testament, Torahnic, as she directly addressed Vose himself.

"Donald Vose, you are a liar, a traitor, a spy," she wrote. "You have lied away the liberty and life of our comrades. Yet not they but you will suffer the penalty. You will roam the earth accursed, shunned and hated; a burden unto yourself, with the shadows of Matthew Schmidt and David Caplan ever at your heels unto the last."[26]

It's unknown whether Donald Vose actually read these words, whether he collected them in his scrapbook of news clipping about the trials and his role in the capture. If he did happen to read them, who knows whether he could consciously grasp the full import of Goldman's curse. His paid protection could not outlast these words. Smoke and drink could not quiet them. These words would hound him, ever trailing him into the future. Soon after these words were published, he was standing on the Municipal Dock in Tacoma, trying to catch a ferry back to Home, and his former comrades, men he had known since childhood, attacked and drove him back to the steamer he'd just left. All he could do to protect himself was cower behind strangers, the ship's crew.

)O(O(

THE FIRST YEAR AFTER GOLDMAN'S CURSE was not entirely bad for Vose. Sure, he couldn't return to Home, but there were other perks for being the star witness in the dynamite cases. The Caplan trial proceeded much like Schmidty's. Vose sat in the courtroom beside Burns and gnawed on unlit cigarettes. He testified against the man he spent long nights talking to, describing how Caplan confessed to helping transport the dynamite used in the bombing, but Caplan appeared more pathetic and less culpable than Schmidty. He seemed to be just a guy who was helping a friend, definitely an anarchist but someone who was unwittingly caught up in a larger plot. And no one could convincingly place him at the scene of the crime. When the case went to the jury, the twelve men deliberated and deliberated. Twice the judge called the men and reminded them of the import of their decision and the high cost of bringing in all of the witnesses. After seventy-six hours, they remained divided, seven for conviction, five for acquittal. When Caplan heard of the hung jury, he smiled broadly with the hope that he'd be acquitted at his next trial.[27]

Immediately after the trial, Vose gave an exclusive interview to the *Seattle Times*. He recapitulated his testimony from the trials but also larded it with accusations and incriminations that seem fabulous and patently untrue. He claimed Caplan had participated in the plot to kill President McKinley. He described a conspiracy to murder John D. Rockefeller by floating a hot air balloon over the oil magnate's Tarrytown mansion and dropping dynamite. He also claimed Schmidty had planned to kill Caplan because the latter missed his family and might squeal.[28] Vose talked and talked, probably only vaguely aware that his words lost their valence with each passing moment. With his cover blown, the only commodity this informant had left was his story, and after the isolation of the trial, he was thrilled to tell it to the eager newsmen and the public. What harm was a little fabrication if it kept all ears trained upon him?

The retrial turned out happily for Vose. Still on the Burns payroll, he had to travel again to Los Angeles. While on the southbound steamer, he befriended a toddler traveling with a nursemaid. Perhaps he was drawn to little Florence Bostrum's openness, her ignorance of his past, her unquestioning acceptance of the bodyguards accompanying him, and during the journey down the coast, the two became boon companions. When Vose arrived in Los Angeles, he met the girl's mother, Jeneva von Kayander Bostrum. The star witness was smitten by the attractive young widow. Throughout the second trial, he called on Bostrum's house regularly. Eventually, she capitulated to his proposals. Vose rushed downtown for a marriage license and then arranged with the district attorney to take leave for a brief honeymoon. The bride hurried to get her ring, an heirloom passed down for two centuries in her family, fitted to her finger. On December 8, 1916, they married in the home of a minister, and the next day the *Los Angeles Times* announced the successful conclusion of their whirlwind courtship.

A week after the wedding, the jury found Caplan guilty of voluntary manslaughter, and the judge sentenced him to ten years in prison. The dynamite trials and their consequences faded from public attention. The romance between Vose and his wife (probably the only one that resulted from "The Crime of Century") was surely brief. In the years to come, all reports of Vose slinking back to Home describe a man alone.

)O(O)(

"AND YOU, GERTIE, unfortunate mother of an ill-begotten son," Emma Goldman wrote. "My heart goes out to you, Gertie Vose. I know you are not to blame. What will you do? Will you excuse the inexcusable? Will you gloss over the heinous? Or will you be like the heroic figure in Gorky's *Mother*? Will you save the people from your traitor son? Be brave, Gertie Vose, be brave!"[29] The article ends with this admonition to an old friend. But what could Gertie Vose really do? The damage had already been done. At best, she could disown her son, let him truly become an exile, but she was reluctant to do even that.

In Donald Vose's story, his mother lingers in the background. Or perhaps she is the background itself. Some who knew her described her as sweet and generous, a devoted mother, but this praise was usually followed by a damning of her son. Others said she didn't have the touch with children. "We kids didn't like her too well because she wasn't really child oriented at all," one family member recalled. "We were just in the way as far as she was concerned."[30] The store owner in Home accused her of being a kleptomaniac, with bars of soap and other small items often disappearing in her pockets. But only mother and son knew the intricacies of their influence upon each other.

After I close the photo album with Donald's Vose's picture, I begin browsing the cabinets of the Key Peninsula Historical Society. A large reproduction of a group portrait of colonists taken in Liberty Hall fills one case. Names are written on the individuals in the portrait, and as I work my way around the photograph, I find Gertie Vose there in the second row, one seat from the end, just behind the kneeling children. Wearing a white blouse, gray hairs threading her curls, she stares at the camera with what appears to be a close-mouthed smile. It is the kind of smile that makes me

Detail showing Gertie Vose,
seated behind kneeling children

feel sad. Would I have the same reaction if I didn't know she was Donald Vose's mother? The photo was probably taken sometime in 1910, years before the betrayal, and yet she already resembles someone who has suffered the incongruities that so often lie between belief and life as it is lived.

When Donald Vose snuck back to Home, his mother did not heed Emma Goldman. She always allowed him to pass over the threshold into her house. Although she received him, surely those four narrow walls could barely contain the conflicting feelings the two felt in each other's presence. It was all the more reason for Vose to root up the handful of old friends who would still drink with him. He stuck to the back paths, cutting through thickets of ferns and brush. When people did encounter him, they mostly ignored him, greeting him with cold glares and silence. One day, however, the Frenchman Gaston Lance walked up to him at a baseball game and spat in his face.[31] Knowing that just about everyone in Home hated him only made Vose thirstier, and eventually it drove him to join the Merchant Marine, to inscribe his unrecognized name upon ships' registers, to become a vagabond upon the earth and sea.

✕❂✕

Still in the saloon, Donald sits beside the man who might understand. Donald's spell in this dive has only deadened his spirit, revealed its bottomless anguish, rather than relieving it as he had hoped. Most people aren't paying attention to him now, but he knows his cue. He slumps on his chair, spent in every way and says, "I may as well confess. There's no lying any more. You know, anyway. I didn't give a damn about the money."

Thinking of his mother, he finally admits: "It was because I hated her."[32]

❈❈❈

IN THE YEARS AFTER DONALD VOSE was outed as an informant and became a star witness in the dynamite trials, his New York drinking buddy Terry Carlin befriended another aimless lush: Eugene O'Neill. In 1915 and 1916, the two palled around, drinking vast quantities of alcohol, haunting the Hell Hole, squatting in vacant apartments, and bumming around the city. As O'Neill embraced Carlin's derelict philosophy and habits, he also listened to the old professional hobo bitterly rehash his role in the capture of Schmidty and defend himself against accusations of being a Burns detective. The two Irish-Americans valued loyalty and would have instinctively reviled the stool pigeon Donald Vose.[33]

Two decades later, after O'Neill became a successful playwright, his memories of listening to the long-winded, circular conversations of pipe-dreaming drunks germinated into what would become his greatest work, *The Iceman Cometh*. A character in the play is directly based on Donald Vose. Dressed as a sport, a young man named Donald Parritt visits Harry Hope's saloon looking for an old companion of his mother's named Larry Slade, who is based on Terry Carlin. Although the particulars of the story have been changed for dramatic effect, the essence of betrayal remains intact: the character has helped police catch his own mother, who was involved in a bomb plot. Donald Parritt wants to confess to what he's done and yearns for sympathy from Slade, but the young man's neediness just makes the elder cranky—it taunts Slade's conviction that he no longer cares about anything. Not until the end of the play can Parritt voice the truth, but speaking it brings no relief. Wordlessly goaded onward by Slade, the poor devil seeks his solace by throwing himself off the roof of Harry Hope's saloon.

The real Donald Vose also died from a fall. On a December night in 1945, he was onboard a ship named the *S. S. Whirlwind*. He was lugging a case of beer up a gangplank, but just as he reached the top, he lost his footing and was suddenly at the mercy of gravity. As he plummeted toward the deck twenty-six feet below, Vose did not know that his literary double, Donald Parritt, will accompany him, again and again, as long as *The Iceman Cometh* is read and performed. "From outside the window comes the sound of something hurtling down, followed by a muffled, crunching thud."[34]

Life at Home: Transportation

MORE THAN ANY OTHER geographic feature, the waterways of Puget Sound instilled a sense of possibility. Home was effectively an island, much like the original utopia imagined by Sir Thomas More. There was no King Utopos to dig up the isthmus of the peninsula, but poor roads, little more than gashes in dense forest, cut off Home from the mainland. All utopias are somehow set apart, either by some physical or temporal distance. Puget Sound with its curving shoreline, backdrop of tall firs, frequently dense and foggy weather, was a microclimate for such schemes. With the perspective reduced to the immediate vicinity of Joe's Bay, dreams could flourish, ebbing and flowing with the tides.

Yet that same water led to many small-scale boating accidents. Gertie Vose and Tom Burns got lost in a November fog and were lucky to be saved before they floated out to sea. Little Lawrence Beck, three and a half years old, could expertly handle his own miniature rowboat, complete with appropriately fitted oars, but once when he was out running an errand for a neighbor, he reached for the candy in his pocket and both oars went overboard and floated out of reach. The rescue party found him drifting near Rocky Point, unconcerned and still sucking a lollypop.

Another time at Rocky Point, the butcher, John Buschi, out on a delivery, cut his launch too close to shore and caught the hull on a submerged rock. No matter how much he shouted and laid on the horn, no one in hearing distance felt kindly enough toward the cantankerous butcher to help. He was stranded three or four hours before the tide would lift him off the rock. It was a long time to reflect on his lack of friends, but the experience only made him more spiteful. Years later, largely on account of his rage, Buschi was locked in the Western State Hospital in Steilacoom. Tears glistened in his eyes when two young men from Home, Radium LaVene and Al Grosse, visited him in the asylum. In his two-year confinement, Buschi told them, only Captain Ed Lorenz had come to see him.

Now, Captain Ed was a beloved man. Everyone sang the praise of the Lorenz steamers—the "slender prow" of the *Typhoon,* the "ponderous sweep" of the *Tyconda*—that ran between Tacoma and Home. On calm crossings, he would lean out of the wheelhouse, a pipe clenched between his teeth, but his dedication was steadfast even in the worst of weather. Colonists never forgot that Captain Ed had carried the first settlers to Home and just about everyone afterward, and according to the collective memory, he saved them from "a mob of drunken hate" after President McKinley's assassination.

The Lorenz steamers structured daily life in Home, and most houses were oriented to see and hear them coming and going. Every morning a horn sounded as the vessel rounded Rocky Point, letting folks know that they had five minutes to rush down to the wharf and catch the boat to Tacoma. Then later in the afternoon, a small congregation formed to greet whatever people or freight arrived upon the steamer. In the summer months, the dock became the haunt of the children, and they were often told to stop swimming and return home for supper when the steamer arrived in the evening.

Donald Vose met such a group of youngsters waiting for the steamer when he pulled to the dock in the *Hoo Doo*. Radium LaVene's father had acquired this trim, white launch in a venture to create a boat service to Seattle, and then hired Vose to operate it. The vessel had come complete with a floating boathouse, but a day or two before, a storm had blown the boathouse from its mooring. In the winds and currents, it had drifted five miles northeast to Horse Head Bay. Leaning on the wheel and squinting in the light, Donald told the gang of kids that was he going to run over and tow the boathouse back. "Who wants to come along?" he asked.

This was B.C. ("before Caplan") recalled Radium LaVene, and Donald was still just another older boy hanging out in Home, so Sylvia and Dave Fox, Ed Halperin, Richie Bowles, and few others climbed onboard. They motored across Carr Inlet and soon found the boathouse. Donald pulled the boat inside, intending to push it back across, but the engine began to sputter and eventually conked out. "Donald cranked and cranked on the fly wheel but no results. Then he started swearing at it, but still no results—finally in desperation he threw a monkeywrench at it a few times, but the engine just didn't want to go. Meanwhile, we drifted back to shore at the little point between Dead Man's Island and Horse Head Bay, just as it was getting dark."

That night, around the bonfire on shore, the castaways sat with empty stomachs and imagined the delicacies everyone was dining upon back at Home. When they grew tired, they waded to the launch and crawled into its bunks. The tide went out while they slept so they awoke lying upon the floor, the launch's hull tilted to one side upon the mud and rocks. In the morning, the famished youngsters dug clams and roasted them upon the fire that Donald had kept burning all night. They remembered Arletta, a small town nearby, and pooled their money, eleven cents in all. Richie Bowles went for food and returned, to the disappointment of the hungry young children, with a sack of Bull Durham tobacco and a big bag of soda crackers.

Unable to fix the engine, the group started out for Arletta. Poison ivy grew along the path. Some of the boys rubbed it on themselves to prove their bravery, but David Fox was terrified of it. Ed Halperin chased him down the trail with a bunch of it.

In Arletta, everyone caught the steamer back to Home. "Most of us were relieved to find that instead of being punished by our parents as we had expected, they were glad to see us—and had secured a small launch and were ready to run across and bring us home if we did not return on the *Tyrus*, as they suspected we might. Our homes, the fireside, our meals and beds were never appreciated as much before as they were that evening. We all felt a little like heroes returning from some great adventure." Except for poor David Fox, who was the only one who broke out in a painful rash on account of the poison ivy.[1]

CHAPTER SIX
Utopia Corrupted

WINTER

EACH OSCILLATION OF THE WIPER BLADE clears a fine sprinkling of rain from my windshield. With the pervasive mist smudging any distinction between earth, water, and air, the westbound Tacoma Narrows Bridge seems a frail tracery of steel, concrete, and cables above a bottomless chasm. The car radio reports that five men have been arrested for stealing the *Arbeit Macht Frei* (*Work Will Set You Free*) sign above the gate to Auschwitz. They had cut it into three pieces and intended to sell it, but no connection to Neo-Nazis is suspected. As I listen to this story, the bridge's expansion joints vibrate the car at regular intervals. Far below, submerged in the depths and resting on a bed of mud, lay the curled girders of the first Tacoma Narrows Bridge, that span that twisted in the wind and then collapsed. I sip my tea and focus on the white stripes of my lane.

Ahead, the bluffs of the Gig Peninsula are serrated with dark conifers. Highway 16 cuts a well-lit path through the maw leading to Purdy, where I'll turn south to the Key Peninsula and head toward Home. In my rearview mirror, dark clouds frame a slit of daylight above Tacoma, where my three-month-old son is sleeping or nursing or crying or maybe even letting a smile take possession of his face. I intended to leave earlier, to be in Home by the first light of the winter solstice, but as I loaded the car, dawn was already seeping in and softening the glow of the inflated Santa Claus in my neighbor's front yard. After the baby yanked me out of my sleep several times, I was too tired to get out the door any sooner. The chronic fatigue of early parenthood sucks like quicksand, mingling with and intensifying any latent doubt. Remind me again why I'm drawn to Home when I could be at my own home today? But I keep my foot on the gas pedal, trying to catch the night, and it keeps slipping away from me toward the Pacific Ocean.

XOXOX

THE LAST OF THE LEAVES were wobbling in the wind outside the Pierce County Superior Court Building on November 19, 1918, the day that a

Panorama of Home from land

complaint was filed against the last holdouts refusing to amicably put an end to the Mutual Home Association. An unremarkable affair—toting a legal document into the stone bulwark of the courthouse and submitting it to the clerk's office to be stamped "filed"—but these papers triggered the final trial of Home.

Only legal professionals could resolve the colony's problems now. The plaintiffs, Thomas J. Mullen and more than thirty other disgruntled residents, were requesting that the court dissolve the Mutual Home Association, sell all the land held in common, and distribute the receipts to the former members. They claimed that the five defendants, a group that included Sylvia Allen and Mattie Penhallow, had usurped control of the organization. According to the complaint, the association itself had ceased to answer the ends of its creation and had been adrift for the past eight years. The only members opposing said dissolution were the defendants.

This was a civil lawsuit, not like the criminal cases where Home was tried for its publications, where the courtroom provided a stage for the defendants to express the justness of their cause. This was more like a divorce involving several dozen people, the translation into legalese of years of discord that

had poisoned the relationships between members of the Mutual Home Association. "Little Groups are standing determined against each other," commented *The Tacoma Times* beneath the headline "Home Colony about to Collapse." "The complaint tells a story of attempted 'steamroller' tactics as one faction tried to gain control of the common lands." Current and former members of the colony, many of whom had once defended the cause of liberty in their writings and even before the courts, now sought to seize power within the association and perhaps profit from it. "The only hope of further success in communistic production there, according to members, lie in the recollection that in previous times, legal squabbles have blown over and members again taken up the plan of 'one for all and all for one.'"[1] Whoever said this to a reporter was blind to the danger in the offing. The successions of previous legal squabbles had left the colony weak and in disrepair, and what approached was more than just another squall. This storm of legal proceedings, of summons and demurrers, affidavits and depositions, receiver reports and court orders would eventually scour Home of its ideals.

XOXOX

PARKED IN THE GRAVEL TURNOUT just before the boat launch at Joe's Bay, I wait for sunrise. A soft light already filters through the banks of clouds, mixing a pale tone into the blur between air, land, and water.

At one time, Home's wharf was right where I sit. Beneath the brambles outside my car are the remains of a foundation and cement retaining wall, and beneath the high tide waters are the stumps of pylons that once supported the wharf that extended out into the water. This is where passengers debarked in Home. Charles W. Johnson was among those that stepped off the steamer in the autumn of 1918. As the receiver for the Pierce County Superior Court, he had been ordered to "bring under his immediate control all moneys, papers, books, records and all other property" of the Mutual Home Association.[2] I imagine a heavyset man with a forgettable, unsmiling face turned toward the thankless task ahead, trudging all over the hillside, taking possession of the fragments of this utopian experiment, perhaps even yanking a big ledger book out of the grip of someone who still wanted the dream to continue.

I'm surprised to hear gravel crunching below tires behind me; I had expected to be alone. A navy blue pickup truck passes and begins backing a steel-bottomed boat on a trailer into the water. "Rip Some Lips" is stenciled in black caps along the boat's gunwale. A tall fishing rod, propped upright on one side, wobbles as the trailer wheels bounce in the ruts. A light but steady wind occasionally builds into a gust, buffeting my car, blowing sprinkles of rain against the windows and shivering the denuded blackberry brambles just outside. It seems an unpleasant day to go fishing.

A man in his late twenties or early thirties gets out of the truck wearing a baseball cap and begins scrambling between his truck and the boat. Beneath his baggy sweatshirt and green waterproof pants, he has the muscular build of someone who works with his body, maybe a construction worker or a firefighter. After he lowers the boat into the water, he can find nothing to tie off to, and the wind keeps pressing the bow away from shore. He approaches my window. "Can you hold the boat for me while I lock up?" he asks.

"Sure. No problem." I get out, walk down to the water, and stand in the wind, holding the yellow line as the boat bobs on the riffles. "What do you catch here?" I ask over the wind, handing the rope back to him.

"Black mouth salmon," he tells me. "We do pretty good out here. It was a warm day, so I figured it would be good. The only thing about warm days is that you get a lot of wind. I haven't been out in a while. I'm not sure what awaits." His eyes shift eagerly away from me toward the water.

The fisherman climbs in the boat, pushes off from shore and drifts out into the bay, behind the blackberry brambles. Back inside my car, out of the wind, I hear his engine fire and see him for a moment bobbing in the swells, white spray blowing across his bow and into his squinting face. I return to writing in my notebook, and then suddenly it seems, he's back on shore, backing his trailer down the ramp and loading his boat. A brown SUV has pulled up, and a thin man in a green uniform steps out. He stands at the top of the boat ramp, talking to the guy who's now throwing things around inside his boat. From the drift of their conversation, it sounds like he had engine trouble. I expect the uniformed man to come talk to me, but he climbs back in his SUV and drives away. When I get out for a walk, the guy has pulled his boat up and he's packing up to leave.

"What happened?" I ask.

"My engine is brand new, never been used, so I didn't think to check it. I got out there and it wasn't working. It's a good thing too because I didn't realize that these were expired," he says, tapping on the license stickers on the side of his boat. "Of course the game warden showed up. But then again, I would have been far from here if the engine was working." He looks at me in my wool cap and raincoat, alone in this place on a desolate Monday morning in December and asks, "What are you doing out here today?" He doesn't seem like the type of guy to ask too many questions, but perhaps all my questions have warmed him up.

Since I've been struggling with a good answer to that question myself, my answer is vague: "I'm doing research about this place."

"Are you thinking of moving out here? Is it for business?"

"I'm interested in the history of the area."

"I can tell you the history in five minutes!" he says and looks at me. I want to ask him to do just that, but he fills in the silence: "I can tell you about the time I got my car stereo jacked out here. But, man, I do love fishing down here. Some people think there's no fish in the South Sound, but that's not true."

)O(O)O(

ONLY WHEN HOME BEGAN TO FAIL did the newspapers refer to it as a utopia. As if to underscore the negative connotations of utopia as an unrealistic vision of society, the headlines read "Corruption in 'Utopia' near Tacoma

Charged" or "Home Colony Utopia about to Collapse." It was as if the newspapers were unconsciously chiding the residents of Home for not understanding that utopia means "no place." But ultimately the press had only a passing interest in the colony's gradual downfall, and the stories flash like a photographer's bulb illuminating only random snapshots of the long, drawn-out fight.

1908. Oscar Engvall and E. B. Berger wait inside the Home Grocery Store located at the end of the wharf. A lantern glows against the neat rows of goods on the shelves, and below the floorboards, water laps at the pilings. Someone has broken into the store several times, but the other general goods store in town, Home Mercantile, remains untouched. They notice a light on inside Engval's empty house up the hill and see a figure ransacking the upper rooms. Engvall and Berger scramble down the dock, up the hill, and catch Richard Gentiss, who later claimed to be a non-member, on his way out. In the tussle, Gentiss's gun goes off, and Berger gets shot in the leg.[3]

1909. Due to the high incidence of burglaries, some of Home's residents request the appointment of a local deputy sheriff. This is but one example of "many methods of higher civilization" the colony has adopted of late, according to the papers. Another includes the platting of the 217 acres situated near Joe's Bay. Most importantly, but to little fanfare, the colony also changes its landholding scheme: "The Mutual Home Association has heretofore held full title to the land, the individual members holding undivided interest in the whole. Each member will now receive his proportionate share of the land."[4]

1911-1912. The fight between the Nudes and the Prudes ignites intense interest. Numerous titillating tales appear of men and women bathing in nothing but water. As the cases drag into the winter, through appeals into the higher courts and debates about who saw what where and when, the cases become a vaudeville act that no one finds funny any more.

1912. The other grocery story in Home, Joe's Bay Trading Company, winds up in court, sued for owing the Mutual Home Association $320.50 in unpaid rent for its twenty-by-thirty-foot space at the end of the wharf.[5]

1916. "Home Colony on Joe's Bay has finally dragged its internal troubles into the open as a long period of wrangling and disagreements culminated with a suit introduced into the superior court today." In the first civil suit, the officers of Mutual Home Association are accused of intermeddling with colony affairs. According to the complaint, the defendants—a group that included Jay Fox and his allies—have seized control of the organization. The plaintiffs want the right to be reinstated as members.[6]

1917. After sorting through the "skein of Home's tangled affairs," including forged entries in the colony's membership roster and in the records of its property holdings, Judge Charles Easterday issues an injunction against Jay Fox and Lewis Haiman, preventing them from taking any part in the Mutual Home Association. All of the officers named in the suit, including colony founder George Allen, are ordered to forfeit their membership.[7]

During its final years Home had a population around three hundred souls but required far more legal counsel than many other small towns. The irony that many outsiders still considered it an anarchist colony was not lost on one contemporary. In a 1915 letter to the weekly labor magazine *Solidarity*, J. C. Harrison described a community that was decidedly not cooperative. Because of its reputation for tolerance, Home had always attracted not just anarchists but proponents of a diversity of political, social, and religious ideas, and yet of late, residents seemed incapable of considering other viewpoints. "Among such a motley assembly," he wrote, "it is not surprising that there are factions and these in turn form two larger parties, the usual radical and conservative groups with their constant quarrels and bickerings which at times amount to nearly open warfare, but generally end in court." Harrison did not recommend anyone turning to an experiment such as Home as an alternative to capitalism. "The colony idea has been exploded often enough to prove that it is no remedy for existing conditions," he concludes.[8]

As the second decade of the twentieth century progressed, many of the stories about Home were buried beneath headlines about the Western Front and hunts for Teutonic Subs. The war erupting in Europe demonstrated the irrelevance of Home. If a utopia couldn't sort out its internal disputes, how could it speak to the world of another, better way?

》○《

THE SUN FINALLY APPEARS as a bright almond-shaped smudge in the clouds, and for a moment, as I walk away from my car, I feel warmth on my face. In the bay, light plays on the wavelets, and several yachts swivel on moorings. Wooden stairways descend from the shore road into water, as if leading to another world that is the inverse of our own but covered in kelp, crabs, and starfish. I turn away, up one of the steep roads perpendicular to the shoreline and lean into the slope. By the time I reach a vantage that takes in much of the bay, the wind has drawn a curtain of clouds across the sky.

Before one house, a wooden sailboat looks as if a record high tide had beached it here a decade ago, a quarter mile from shore, a hundred feet above sea level. In another yard, I find a dinghy so top heavy with grass that it looks like it would capsize if it weren't so firmly planted in the ground. People have disappeared inside their homes on this winter day, or they are busy going someplace else. I keep noticing "No Trespassing" and "Private Property" signs guarding beach-front access, vacant lots, and stands of second-growth trees.

Only a couple of the old-growth stumps remain as swellings in the soil. Although I seek these traces of history in the landscape, my attention is drawn to the tall trees that were probably seeded soon after the land was cleared a century ago. The twisted, moss-covered limbs of the deciduous trees sway and rattle. The shiny leaves of the holly trees jounce the crimson berries, flaunting the only color besides green or gray around. The towering Douglas firs wave branches like the arms of a kid spinning a hula-hoop. Cedar trees hang their needles like sodden, upside down ferns flapping.

SPRING

MIST RISES OFF JOE'S BAY, drifting toward the lower pressure in the open water. Or maybe this is the slight exhalation of the trees. It's nearly nine o'clock, and I've got an hour before I meet Lorraine, the first person I'll meet who lives in Home. A mutual friend introduced us.

It's hard to believe that the waters of Joe's Bay glimmering in the sun have also known the rages of Pacific storms and waves that could crush my car, but it is the proximity to the ocean that accounts for the mild winters and long, gentle springs at this latitude. Even though today is the vernal equinox, daylight already seems to have the upper hand. Leaf buds haven't begun to dot the branches of the trees, but up the hill, pale pink flowers canopy the magnolias. In only a few days, the wilting petals will carpet the ground beneath, giving way to the cherry trees, the next to bloom in the parade of flowers that processes from early March to late June.

Often, I can only note the evidence of change taking place, barely aware of the powerful forces at work beneath. My infant son is a different person than he was when I last visited here. His growth and development have happened right before my eyes, but I seem only able to recognize them in hindsight, as I reflect on them or scroll through photographs. He now sits up, grabs things, babbles, laughs, and we're trying to teach him to wave. As I left this morning, my wife took his hand and guided it through motion, saying "Bye, bye, Daddy. Bye, bye, Daddy," and he just stared at me, not yet grasping what it means to come or go.

Most of history happens when we're not paying attention, and the major events, the notches on the timeline, call us to attention. Surrounding the pivotal moments are an infinite number of ordinary moments, like this one where I sit in my car, thinking of my son at home and waiting to meet someone who lives in Home. Mist now rises straight off the water. Something splashes—a fish jumping? a bird diving?—and rings spread out through the water, the sunlight forming constellations.

✕✕✕

ALL OF THE LEGAL DISPUTES originated in two amendments to the bylaws passed in 1908 and 1909. The first allowed members to own the fee simple title to their own land, and the second stated that if the property was sold, the certificate of membership in the Mutual Home Association would not pass on to the new owner.

Prior to these changes, all land was held in common by the Mutual Home Association and the residents owned whatever improvements they made to the land. In the early days, this arrangement tended to attract like-minded people to the experiment and winnowed out those with mixed motives or only a passing interest. But afterward, when people owned their land outright, then anyone could move to Home for any number of reasons, one of the most attractive being cheap goods and land. It is then no coincidence that the Nudes and the Prudes episode erupted immediately after this change.

But why would the members change the scheme in the first place? It was as if these anarchists forgot Prodhoun's famous aphorism: "Property is theft!" Take away the landholding scheme and the Mutual Home Association was a mere legal entity, weaker than the paper its charter was written on. Without the landholding scheme, Home became nothing more than another small town.

The historical record leaves a lot of room for speculation. The bylaws were amended during the lag between the last issue of *The Demonstrator* in the winter of 1908 and the first issue of *The Agitator* in 1910, and none of the local Tacoma newspapers reported it. Stewart Holbrook, a journalist who visited Home in the 1930s and interviewed residents who lived there through that time, wrote that the issue divided the community: "Some wished to continue the Mutual Home Association, which held the title to the colony's land, while others wanted a deed to their acres. Considerable squabbling went on and there were some rather hot meetings in Liberty Hall, but on the whole they appear to have settled their differences with less rancor than is common."[9] Given the rancor that followed, it is questionable whether the colonists "settled their differences," but the community did ultimately agree on one thing: to alter the landholding scheme. Any change to the original bylaws of the Mutual Home Association required a unanimous vote, and then once the bylaws were amended, almost everyone in the colony took the opportunity to own the land outright. The complaint filed in the Superior Court in 1918 contains this revealing sentence: "Within a year after November 23, 1908, practically all of said holders of Association membership certificates exchanged the same for or had issued them in lieu of regular Association deeds under the terms and conditions provided for in the Amendments."[10]

But this still doesn't answer the question: Why? The court documents hint at practical concerns, of people not wanting to pay taxes on land they did not own. Many of the original settlers had died or moved on, and those that remained had perhaps lost the zeal of youthful idealism. George Allen, one of Home's founders, was in a fever to prove his patriotism, buying up Liberty Bond after Liberty Bond to support the war effort, while up the hill Liberty Hall stood silent and derelict, most of its windows broken into shards.

Another founder of Home, Oliver Verity, noted in 1915 how much the colony had drifted in a letter to Eugene Muirhead, who had visited the experiment in its early days. "Home is not like it was when you were here," wrote Verity. Now separated from his wife and living in Santa Cruz, California, he followed Home's affairs through his daughter, who had stayed in Home and married James Govan. "Some of the vital tenets of Home remain in vogue. But the landholding scheme has been largely abolished. And they hold individual deeds. That was a jar to me to have them go back to private ownership, a scheme that has long proven itself rotten as far as the laboring man was concerned."[11] But it's easy to criticize from afar: he had abandoned the experiment by 1908, so he was not there to cast a dissenting vote.

)O(O(

As WE WALK THROUGH HER BACK YARD, I ask Lorraine about an old foundation covered with blackberry brambles and filled with a pile of stones. She doesn't know what might have been there: she and her husband have only lived in Home for four years, renting this house on B Street at the top of the hillside, overlooking Joe's Bay. Her land is still in the original two-acre parcels that members received when they joined the Mutual Home Association. Brush covers most of the sloping property, but just below Lorraine's home is a large clearing. As we approach, I see rounded stones and bits of driftwood laid in large concentric circles in the moss and tufts of grass. "Is that a labyrinth?" I ask.

"Yes. It's a seven circuit Celtic labyrinth," Lorraine tells me. "Every Memorial Day I clean it up and walk it, thinking about all of the soldiers who have died. It's all overgrown now. I need to clean it off." The labyrinth seems like some kind of sign I must reckon with. Of their own volition, my feet wander into the entrance, and before I know what I'm doing, I'm taking a curved route through shaggy turf and the brown, desiccated stalks of Queen Anne's lace and hemlock.

Lorraine enters the labyrinth behind me. When I reach the top of the first circuit, I gaze down at a hunk of pink rock placed among the gray stones. "That's rose quartz. It marks due east, the direction of the mountain," Lorrain says, referring to Mount Rainier.

The quartz also marks the direction of the Odell house, just across the bay. This to me seems like another sign, that one of the first houses built in

Odell Welcome
Cottage

Home is visible from her property. Before coming, I had closely investigated an old photograph of the Odell house, and there the house is. It looks different than it did a century ago, when the wilderness seemed on the verge of swallowing the structure. Now painted white, with red shutters, it is surrounded by a well-kept lawn. While we were sitting on the porch a bit earlier, Lorraine wondered who lives in the Odell house now, whether they're old timers or someone who kept it in the family.

As I walk the labyrinth, each circuit getting me closer to the center, we talk less, but the words of the conversation we just had rattle around in my head. The first thing she said: "I feel like I live in paradise." As we spoke, I wanted to record her words because they might capture something of the people who live in Home now, but when I arranged to meet Lorraine, I'd only asked to chat with her, not interview her, so I kept my notebook closed. Now as I step, her words get jumbled in my mind as I attempt to inscribe them on my memory.

"I need earth, water, and sky." Step. "This is a healing place." Step. "My daughter has Lyme Disease. We try to teach people around here about it." Step. "I was looking for a place without stairs and a view of the water. It's not much to look at," she said, pointing to the double-wide behind us, "but look at where it is." Step. "Some people who don't know the area think there's just a bunch of meth addicts who live out here, but it's not as bad as it was." Step. "People here are grounded. The natural world puts their lives in context. It's hard to worry about your life and your problems when you've got this to look at." She gestured toward the bay where she's seen eagles and osprey vie with the gulls and crows. "I'm an old hippie who chose it as a lifestyle. Most of us who live out here scrape by." She lists her various jobs: jazz singer, blogger for a local newspaper, and minister for the Universalist Church. "I hear it was wild out here in the seventies. This place has always attracted people who want to live alternative lifestyles."

"I'm a spore borne on the wind, and I've lived all over." Her dark hair peppered with gray is braided loosely behind her head, with the loose strands forming a halo. She squinted toward the water and told me: "I've only been here for four years, but I don't want to go anywhere. I could stay here the rest of my life. If we had enough money, we'd buy this property."

As I continue through the labyrinth, the conversation falls away, and my thoughts turn inward. Out of habit, I think of history spatially as a left-to-right chronology of events. This happened, then that happened. But it occurs to me that the experience of history more closely resembles the labyrinth. The elements of the past collide to create the present, all the facts swirling together. Today is the seventh anniversary of the invasion of Iraq. This is the equinox, but the sun has not yet reached its zenith. My shadow slants up the slope. Somewhere on this hill lives a ninety-five-year-old woman, the granddaughter of Sylvia Allen, who has collected reams of documents on Home's history. Magnolias blossom on barren branches. Step over the dry umbel of another tilting Queen Anne's lace. Or is it the skeleton of the poisonous water hemlock?

The journey goes much faster than I expected, and I'm at the center before I know it. The path stops in a blunt round of stones, not a dead end but a living end. Lorraine speaks. "A three-year-old asked me when he got here, 'What is this?' 'It's the center of the universe,' I told him and he went, 'Aww!' You know, you've got to tell them stories."

)O(O(

AS THE FINAL TRIAL OF HOME worked its way through the Pierce County Superior Court in 1918 and 1919, the list of parties in the filed complaint expanded to include a good proportion of the colony. The list of defendants grew to thirteen people in all, including Jay Fox, Louis Haiman, and George Allen. The plaintiffs, represented by Thomas Mullen, also numbered thirteen, but over thirty more people added their names as interveners in the litigation because they had a stake in the ultimate decision.

The court documents, especially the ever-growing complaint, reveal just how much enmity existed in Home. All of the property owned by the association—Liberty Hall, the sea wall, the sidewalks, the cemetery—was dilapidated, the spirit of volunteerism long since snuffed by the disputes. The two factions had elected two competing sets of officers for the Mutual Home Association, so that no one knew who ultimately was responsible. And the defendants, a group that included colony founders and vocal advocates for freedom of speech and action, assumed a role not unlike an abusive husband who cannot comprehend why his wife has filed for divorce. To maintain a semblance of control, they forged documents, held secret meetings, issued memberships and property deeds to individuals who had been court ordered to refrain from participating in association affairs, and they resolutely refused to admit that the experiment was failing.

"The purpose of the Association is to assist its members in obtaining and building homes for themselves and to aid in establishing better social and moral conditions," stated the Mutual Home Association's articles of incorporation, but for the plaintiffs, many of whom were either the adult children of colonists or more recent residents, the association was dead and had been for nearly fifteen years. "The continuous strife and hostility among members of said Association has contributed to the denigration of social and moral conditions," argued the complaint. "To continue would only make the situation worse."[12]

On September 10, 1919, Judge Ernest Card ruled in favor of the plaintiffs. In his decree, Card described the association as "wholly impotent to perform or accomplish its charter purposes." He ordered that the Mutual Home Association be "dissolved and that its business affairs … be wound up, its property sold and after the payment of its indebtedness and the costs and expenses of this proceedings and the receivership herein, that its proceeds thereafter remaining be distributed among its members."[13] With the issue of this order, the experiment ended, but the trial wasn't entirely over.

)O(O(

I SLOWLY DRIVE MY CAR along A Street, trying to absorb one last view of the sun glinting on the water. At 6th Avenue, I turn to pass a front-gabled A-frame house with a dinghy in the yard that is filled with long stalks of grass. It has become a landmark for me and a site I return to on each visit. On my last visit to the local library, I came across a survey and inventory of Home by the Pierce County Historic Preservation Program. From it, I learned that Sylvia Retherford, a descendant of George and Sylvia Allen, lives at this address. Lois Waisbrooker once owned the lot, and there is a well on the property reputed to be hers. Retherford has become a local historian, and several libraries in the region hold copies of the extensive collection of documents she accumulated and bound together in five volumes. She is ninety-five years old, and as far as I know, still living. Each time I pass the grass-filled dinghy, I hope to see a small, elderly woman walking gingerly in her garden, but today I see no one. The windows in the house are dark.

The engine shifts gears to climb the slope, and at the top, I turn right. Lorraine told me that the mountain could be seen from the top of 10th Avenue and gave me directions on how to get there, but I've become familiar enough with the street grid to know that I can just zigzag my way there. As I follow the lattice of roads right and left, it strikes me that one of the pieces of evidence to Home's demise is right beneath the tires of my car. "The plat map filed with the county in 1909 is both a summary of the physical plan of Home and an instrument for its conversion, later, of the communitarian structure of landholding to a system of private ownership," wrote the investigators in the historic survey.[14] The combined decision to alter the landholding scheme and then to have the community platted fundamentally altered the colonists' relationship not only to the land but to each other. With these actions, they took a fateful step toward the "Private Property" and "No Trespassing" signs that now command all visitors to obey the boundary lines of the parcels.

I reach 10th Avenue and turn right, and drive down a short ways, and there it is, the white, slouching peak of Mount Rainier. Under the disorienting influence of the trees, hills, and inlets, I had not expected it to be in that direction. I want to stay, to spend more time looking at the mountain, to investigate the flowering trees, to follow the course of the grid on the hillside with my feet, but I've got to get to the historical society. Musty documents, yellow photographs, and a headache wait for me.

Summer

I close my car door and begin strolling along A Street in Home, away from the boat ramp. The low tide has exposed the shallows, and in the distance, the shapes of a deer and fawn slowly work their way across the expanse of green seaweed, trying to find footing among the rocks. Over the dark water hangs a low bank of clouds. Today doesn't feel like the summer solstice, that there are fifteen hours of daylight. Like many days this spring, the drizzle last night gave way to the shades of gray reminiscent of old black and white photographs. I doubt that the sun will burn off the clouds today or in the days ahead pull the season toward warmer, drier weather.

I stop briefly, as I often do on my visits, at the historical marker in front of the Dadisman's brick house. I often notice little quirks in the facts listed there, and today I wonder why Philip Van Buskirk, the retired sailor who briefly visited Home, is included among "Members of the Mutual Home Association and other early pioneers of the Home community." He didn't exactly get along with his hosts and spent most of his short time here escaping to Lakebay for booze and smokes. At least the memory of Van Buskirk has found the abode he yearned for while alive but was too stubborn and restless to accept.

I hold in my hands *An Automobile Tour through Key Peninsula History* published by the Key Peninsula Historical Society. It has a decent map of Home, and on it, there are a number of sites I want to locate. I begin winding my way on foot up the hill. In a two-track driveway sits a little brown rabbit. For a moment, I wish my son was here so that I could point it out to him. Today is Monday, normally the day that I stay home and care for him. Although it is refreshing to get some leave from my parental responsibilities, I miss him. Sure, there are those trying times, but somewhere in the grueling routine of sleepless nights, warming bottles, and changing diapers, I have begun to harbor a love that fundamentally alters everything.

I'm learning how much effort goes into creating a home for a child and how it brings moments of unrefined joy, such as when the baby smiles, revealing the two small teeth that just poked through his gums, and says, "Da! Da! Da!" I encourage him to say "Dada," in a half-joking attempt to cajole a name for myself from the baby talk. From his high chair, yogurt dripping down his chin, he looks at me like I'm speaking nonsense: everything is "da! da!" right now.

Home Colony members in Liberty Hall

The whine of brakes pulls me out of my thoughts. I step to the side of the road as a green dump truck barrels down a dark passageway through the trees, the branches above convulsing in the wind it creates. The garbage men are the first people I've seen today. They stop, the mechanical arm jerks the can up to the receptacle, and the bags thud inside. I'm sure my son would delight in this too.

When I reach the place on the map marking the Vose house at 9th and B, I admire the pink dogwood and the last of the rhododendrons in bloom, but my untrained eye cannot determine what of the attractive, green Craftsman before me is original. Up the hill, on 11th and C, at the Miles house, a black and white dog barks viciously behind the wire fence, discouraging lingering. Next door a Rottweiler growls, and I cross the street. Farther on, four goats in a field munch on grass near snarled and mossy fruit trees that look ancient but were probably planted by settlers. Without wind, the smell of cut wood drifts up the hill and voices carry from as far away as across the bay.

I turn to follow 11th to the end, seeking the place I've wanted to see more than any other, but when I reach the spot on the map for Liberty Hall, black plastic slats threaded through a six-foot-tall chain link fence block the view. More than any other structure in Home, Liberty Hall represented the spirit of the colony, and I'd hoped to view some remnant, perhaps the outline of a foundation. But I see nothing but brush and tree trunks through the narrow slats.

)O(O(

THE NIGHT IT BURNED, Liberty Hall illuminated the darkness with a crackling orange glow. The inferno inhaled through the gaping, broken windows and exhaled upward through the rafters. The flames consumed walls, floorboards that had thudded with dancing feet. How many talks, how many meetings, how much laughter, how many songs had once filled its rooms? It was the last place where Home's residents could have sorted out their differences. The heavy beams, hewn from old-growth timber, eventually collapsed inside, and the conflagration exploded. Cinders swarmed like hornets in the updraft.

While it's unlikely that a fire brigade formed to haul water up from the bay, it seems clear that someone set Liberty Hall on fire soon after Judge Card dissolved the Mutual Home Association. Charles W. Johnson had written to the judge about a "building known as Liberty Hall, which for the past three years, has been condemned as being unsafe; that it is now in dilapidated condition and its only value consists in what lumber might be salvaged therefrom which is estimated not to exceed $50.00."[15] Johnson had succeeded in selling Liberty Hall to a local resident for scrap lumber, but before the $110 check was deposited and the boards pried apart, the building burned under mysterious circumstances.

The dry receivership reports do not speculate on arson, but those involved in the trial would have known about the $250 fire insurance policy taken out on the building. Perhaps one of the plaintiffs in the settlement hoped to get more money out of the derelict building, but if that was the case, the conclusion of the receiver's work only brought disappointment. In the final report, filed April 19, 1921, the entirety of the Mutual Home Association's assets—an amount equaling $2,314.53, collected from selling commonly held land, the fire insurance, and even the sale of a phonograph for $12.50—went toward legal expenses. Charles W. Johnson received $500 for his services, while the attorney representing the plaintiffs, Henry Arnold Peterson, was paid $1,676.53, the remaining sum after covering all other expenditures.

)(O)(O)(

As I WALK DOWN THE HILL, I walk past the dinghy converted to a planter without noticing it. In the months since my last visit, the grass has grown so long that it hangs over the gunwales and conceals the boat beneath. Only when I reach A Street and turn around do I realize my mistake, and I return to stare at the little vessel for a while, reflecting on how the once watertight hull is now becoming the soil it holds.

Each time I've come here, I had hoped to catch a glimpse of Sylvia Retherford. She seems like the perfect person to talk to, but now I know why I've never seen her. Joyce Neiman, the president of the Key Peninsula Historical Society, recently told me that Sylvia (or Stella, as her friends call her) has Alzheimer's and has been in a nursing home for a few years now. "The best thing to look at would be the documents she collected," Joyce said.

I have gotten a sense of her quirky and energetic personality from working my way through her *Compilation of Writings and Photos Concerned with the History of Home, Washington*, which encompasses a staggering amount of source material: old issues of *New Era* and other Home publications, newspaper clippings, personal reminiscences of growing up in Home, countless photographs, court documents, published and unpublished scholarly articles. For all its wealth, her compilation is also somewhat baffling. Anything related to Home could end up in the binders, such as high school papers, and for some reason, a pamphlet on jellyfish, but the randomness is charming. A boundless love of Home and a voracious curiosity seem to be the organizing principles.

As I look at Retherford's A-frame house, I wonder if her documents remain inside. I regret that I can't sit down with her and wade through them. As much information as her compilation provides, it also raises questions. In the profiles I've read of her, she presents herself as knowing "what really happened" in Home's past, her knowledge acquired not just from research but also from stories passed down in the family. If I could, I'd ask her about where she heard the story about Ed Lorenz saving the colony from the Loyal League. I'd ask her: Why did Home fail? And what, if anything, of those days of animosity and infighting was passed down in her family lore?

Now that I know that the house is uninhabited, I can spot the clues. Grass at the edges of the mowed lawn grows long, untrimmed by a weed whacker, and there are no freshly planted flowers. On my visit to the Key Peninsula Historical Society this past spring, I met two elderly volunteers who had known Stella in the Garden Club. "Remember her?" the woman asked her friend. "She used to have such a beautiful garden."

)0(0(

O*N PAPER AT LEAST,* the experiment in Home failed just as it reached the dividing line between successful and unsuccessful utopias described by sociologist Rosabeth Moss Kanter. In one of the few systematic studies on the successes and failures of nineteenth-century utopias, she suggests that viable communities last longer than twenty-five years, the length of a generation. In her analysis, Kanter raises an important question that all such communities must answer: "In utopia … who takes out the garbage?"[16] She means this literally, but her question illustrates the problem at the heart of all such utopian endeavors. As the community seeks to implement an ideal, how will it accommodate the junk that participants bring or create while carrying out the utopian vision? If not properly sorted, disposed of, or transformed into compost, these byproducts of humans living in close proximity can poison the community.

Kanter seems to think that all successful utopias are alike, while all failed utopias are unhappy in their own way. Since success to her means long-lived, she identifies six commitment mechanisms that sustained successful communities: sacrifice, investment, renunciation, communion, mortification, and transcendence. As her choice of terms indicates, these communities, such as the Shakers or Oneida, all had a religious bent. Since these communities tended to be highly structured, often organized around a single charismatic leader, they were so unlike Home that the question of why Home failed no longer seems like the right one to ask. Instead, if Home had so few of Kanter's commitment mechanisms, perhaps a better question is: How did it last so long?

In its early days, Home did have a few commitment mechanisms, at least to a degree. In the pioneering phase, members were forced to make both a sacrifice and an investment to join the experiment: they had to travel, often across the country, and then clear the land and build their own house. These activities did not leave much time and energy for doubt and resentment. But just as the community was getting established, perhaps comfortable even, right around the turn of the twentieth century, Home experienced the most significant commitment mechanism: communion as a result of persecution. "Persecution serves several functions for communion and cohesiveness," writes Kanter. "Facing a common enemy binds people together, such integration being one of a number of functions of social conflict."[17] Perhaps the hostile Tacoma newspapers and the Loyal League did Home a favor when they rallied against the colony after the McKinley assassination. After that event, Home had to prove to an observing public that it could succeed.

While external forces may have promoted its longevity, sometime in the first decade of the twentieth century, even before the infighting erupted, Home ceased to fulfill its charter purpose "to establish better social and moral conditions." E. E. Slosson, a sociologist who visited Home in 1903, in many ways predicted its demise:

> As the spirit of devotion and self-sacrifice possessed by the founders of
> socialistic communities declines, as to a certain extent it must decline, and
> the novelty wears off and the ideal becomes commonplace, laziness, envy
> and malice will no longer appear in abeyance, and as others come in who
> are not inspired with the original enthusiasm, or are naturally depraved and

not amenable to the milder forms of social control, it seems that more rules will have to be made and enforced.[18]

Because most people in Home were constitutionally averse to rules or the imposition of their values on their neighbors, they were unable to adopt shared practices that sustained their community values in the face of inertia, complacency, and self-interest. The anarchist colony at Home was born in contradiction: it was a collective of individuals seeking absolute freedom. When its members chose to own the land outright, rather than in common, they unwittingly abandoned the very principle that held together the Mutual Home Association. With this change, the articles of incorporation became an empty legal contract, unfit for the conflicts ahead. There was little to bind together the members of the community beyond their proximity to each other.

✕✕✕

I'VE RENTED A KAYAK from a guy named Kelly in Lakebay who has a spray-painted sign advertising his business in his driveway, and we're now riding in his truck toward Penrose State Park, following a road that burrows through the thick trees. Behind the wheel, Kelly wears a camo baseball cap and a T-shirt with a buxom woman in a bikini made out of Confederate flags. Kelly's not much of a talker and neither am I, but I try to make conversation: "How's business this summer?"

"This weather has been killing me," he says. "You're my first customer." I had offered him another first when we were going over the rental agreement on the porch outside his doublewide. I asked about the clause saying that the renter could not paddle into restricted areas, and he told me, "You're the first person to ask about that. That's there so you don't try to paddle to Gig Harbor." I'd just wanted to make sure that it would be all right to paddle over to Home instead of around Penrose, as most people do.

We park in the lot above the boat launch, hoist the orange Old Town kayak out of the back of his truck, and carry it down a steep path to the pebbly shore of Mayo Cove. I drag the kayak into the water and climb in. As I paddle away, the shallow bottom rolls beneath me, gently dropping off until the water darkens to the color of oil. The surface has a viscous, filmy quality, and it feels like the hull should just glide across. As I pass a narrow spit, the bottom rises again, this time speckled with sand dollars.

My shoulders, unaccustomed to paddling, ache at first, but I settle into a steady pace. Rounding the point, I pass docks and boats, houses and cabins barely visible in the trees. As I get just inside the bay, I stop paddling and pull out my lunch. I bite into my sandwich. Nearby a tiny shell floats on the surface of the water, and now that I'm not moving, I feel as liable to tip as it does, though I suspect it would be difficult to overturn this wide vessel. Something breaks the surface of the water in the distance, but gulls swoop over the area and all I see are concentric circles rippling across the water.

In the distance floats a neglected sailboat, its shrouds a snag of cables gently slapping the mast, a bright line of algae appearing on its hulls as it rocks in the gentle swell. The hillside rises above it, looking not much different than any other inhabited shoreline along Puget Sound, yet this landscape was the scene of the tragicomedy—or was it the comitragedy—of the birth and death of a utopia. It didn't exactly collapse, though. After the receiver finished his work and the last of the communally owned property transferred into private hands, the hillside looked no different to the steamer pulling up to the wharf. Mothers' voices still carried down to their children playing on the beach or out rowing in the bay, calling them home for dinner.

My lunch finished, I pick up my paddle and turn. Two dark eyes stare at me, hovering just above the water about twenty feet away. I turn for a better look, but the dark dome of the sea lion's head submerges in a blink.

Autumn

A MAN STANDS DOWN at the water's edge, drinking beer out of a paper sack and occasionally chucking stones into Joe's Bay. A warm September day, high banks of scalloped clouds span the sky above and beyond the hills cumulous billow on the horizon. The past few days brought sun, the first seen in a while, but the rain has given a preview of what's to come. By this equinox, night has already shown its dominance over the season to come. The man walks up to the cement boat ramp, and as he passes where I sit against the break wall, I ask, "How's it going?"

"Pretty go-ood!" he says with a smile and sense of finality that seem to indicate he's not interested in saying anything else. Not that I'm interested in talking much either. I've been feeling sluggish, not quite up to unearthing the details of this last episode of Home. My attention is divided between the demands of caring for an infant and piecing together the fragments of history about Home. The constant fatigue, like a chill, has penetrated to my core, but like a participant in a utopian experiment myself, I've already invested too much to give up now. With all my ambivalence, I wait to meet Evelyn Evans, who may be the last person alive who personally knew and can remember the founders and participants in Home.

My son will celebrate his first birthday in a few days. A couple times my wife has said, "I used to think that my birthdays were just for me, but they were for my parents too." We've got a baby book that catalogs his milestones over the past year. Nowadays, we're paying attention to his ability to communicate with baby sign language. His favorite word is "light," expressed by squeezing the fingers and thumb into a point and then opening them like dispersing rays, and he sees them everywhere. "Yes, that's a light," we say to him. Harder to notice is how all of this transforms me: how those kisses on top of his fuzzy head, how the broken nights of sleep, how the grind of his crying face against my chest, how the frequent interruptions as I sit at the computer writing, how the whole incomprehensible experience of parenthood edges me, if at times reluctantly, toward greater maturity.

Why would I choose such a time to take on such an unwieldy project? I am creating a home for a little boy while I've tried to recover what happened in Home. Yet this past year, caring for an infant, has taught me more about the sacrifices those early founders made to establish Home than all of my research. Since his conception and birth, I've painted walls, spread soil and seed in the backyard, torn down and built a fence, all so that he would have safe place to play and grow. Knowing nothing of my sweat and sore muscles, he will take all of this for granted, as the way things are, as I did with the places I called home as a child.

I stand and walk toward the water. Across the bay, a circular saw whines through boards. Above, crows and gulls circle and hammer out calls. I stoop to examine a massive jellyfish, the size of a large pizza, sprawled on the shore. A small pebble rests on the top, as if someone put it there. Stones show through the edges of the flattened bell, where it thins into translucent brown and pink gelatin. Is it still alive? Or has it already passed in silence? Will the tide lift it from shore and wash it out into deeper water?

I follow the boat ramp up toward my car and stop to read a new sign, posted since my last visit. With a skull and crossbones, it reads "Danger Toxic Shell Fish" and warns that the clams, oysters, and mussels should not be consumed because they contain a paralytic chemical. One can still eat the blackberries though, and they are in season. The bushes right next to where everyone parks have been stripped clean, but farther on, vines crowd the whole strip above the beach, hanging with an embarrassing abundance of dark berries, ready for the picking.

ⅩⵔⅩ

WHAT IS THE VALUE OF UTOPIA, if it inevitably tends toward failure? The word utopia has become synonymous with the impractical, foolish, and unrealistic. Having observed how the utopian impulse can swiftly and fatally turn dystopian, as it often did in the twentieth century, some would argue that utopia is inherently dangerous. Leave such visions to the pages of literature.

But utopia reminds us that human society is constructed in part by our own agreement to participate in it. Utopia posits the radical notion that through our ingenuity and imagination we might create a new and better way of organizing ourselves. The founders and the participants in Home dared to consider a different way of relating to each other, and in doing so created a little bubble of the future on the backwaters of Puget Sound. Many of the ideas they argued and fought for became commonplace later in the twentieth century. Sexual practices aside, the notion of free love—that a union should be based upon love and freely chosen—has become, for better or worse, the widely accepted underpinning of all unions. And what about all of those single mothers living without judgment on the hill above Joe's Bay? And the food fads, the yoga classes, the liberal attitudes toward child rearing, the arguments in favor of free speech? A time traveler from twenty-first century America would not find the residents of Home very shocking.

None of these qualities were unique in and of themselves. Many of these ideas did not originate in Home; they were borrowed from other late nineteenth- and early twentieth-century radicals. But for a time, Home was a place where unconventional ideas were welcome and could flourish, even when individuals could not agree. And perhaps in their failure, too, they left a gift, demonstrating just how difficult it can be to maintain such open-mindedness and civility.

If there is a fatal flaw to utopia, it is that true believers attempt to enact a vision born of the mind, of reason, to address the deepest yearnings of the human heart: to find a home. A community must find a way for individuals to sacrifice limited self-interest for the long-term collective good and yet remain fully engaged, happy participants in the whole. In Home, individual freedom remained a principle fiercely defended against all else, and it ultimately unleashed the destructive forces of fear and anger that remain latent in all human organizations.

))())(

"I NEARLY SHOPPED TILL I DROPPED," Evelyn Evans says. "I was so bushed I had to take a nap." She's ninety-one years old and lives alone, but every Wednesday a woman helps her with groceries, and today she had to rest, which explains why she didn't answer the phone when I called earlier at regular intervals between 3:30 and 5:00 p.m. I worried that we wouldn't be able to talk today, that perhaps the joke she made when we arranged this meeting had come true. When I suggested that we meet in a week, she'd said with a laugh, "I hope I'm still here!"

We sit in her living room facing each other, me on the couch, she on the love seat, at a distance that feels a little uncomfortable at first. The room has a stillness that only the aged can impress upon a space, the quiet of a church or archives, where order reigns and every object appears to have settled into its appropriate place. There is a slight trace of an air freshener similar to the one my own grandmother used, but before I can detect its elements, it has faded into the background.

Evelyn has a thin frame, short white hair, and glasses. As she begins telling me about the past, her voice is deep and clear, and often broken by an easy laugh. Her grandfather was Martin Dadisman, the wealthy Virginian who donated land to the colony in the early days. Her father David Dadisman ran the store in Home for many years, and when I specifically ask about the anarchist days, she says, "Dad didn't get involved in colony business, so I don't really know."

Although the Mutual Home Association ended right around the time Evelyn was born, she remembers details that didn't end up in newspaper articles and history books, such as the terrifying darkness between the slats of the stairs on Commercial Dock in Tacoma. When the Lorenz steamer landed in Tacoma, everyone had to climb a series of stairs up from the wharf to the city. Looking down between the boards, Evelyn could see the water getting farther and farther away and disappearing in the shadows below. "It seemed like it was forever," she says.

She describes the egg-candling business that thrived briefly in Home in the 1930s. I have to ask exactly what egg candling was, and she explains that they'd hold eggs up to a bright flame to see whether they had been fertilized, then they'd package and ship the eggs to Tacoma and points beyond. "We did very well for a while. Then the business ended and everybody lost their shirts."

As a girl, Evelyn lived for a few weeks with Jay Fox and his second wife, Cora, when her brother had scarlet fever. By that time Jay was a slim, white-haired old fellow. "He was gentle natured," she says. There was a man who stayed with them named Padgum. "I don't know what his story was, where he came from, but he candled eggs and lived with the Foxes." She gets up, goes to the china cabinet, and pulls out a plate with a rose in the center. It was hand-painted by Cora Fox.

Several times as we talk, she speaks of Sylvia Retherford. "Stella could tell you that," but then she acknowledges that her mind is gone. "There are getting to be fewer and fewer of us around who remember the way it was."

"Who else is there?"

"Honestly, I can't tell you." She mentions a friend nearby, now confined to a wheelchair, but she hasn't spoken to her in months. "I guess I'm the only one who's still talking a lot." She laughs. The sound is loud and sharp and could almost be mistaken for a sob. "It's sad," she admits.

)O(O(

OVER THE TWENTIETH CENTURY, Home became a great human-interest story. The once reviled collective of anarchists had transformed itself into an attractive rural community with substantial homes and bounteous orchards and gardens, but what drew journalists from both local and national newspapers to the settlement out on the Key Peninsula was its past. Early on, the curious could find many people who still recalled those days.

In 1937, Stewart Holbrook, writing for the *The Oregonian*, found Lewis Haiman in his barbershop on the waterfront. The former president of the Mutual Home Association was now sixty-two years old. A photograph of Abner Pope hung on the wall, and from it, the white-bearded anarchist of yesteryear gazed down on the men getting their hair trimmed and faces lathered and shaved. "I have had no reason to change my political beliefs in the past thirty-seven years," Haiman told the reporter. "Life at Home has allowed everything I could ask—a decent living, in good times and bad; plenty to read; excellent neighbors; and more freedom than I have seen elsewhere. I don't think there is much else in life."[19]

A photograph in the article shows George Allen, then age seventy-seven, in robust health, dressed in overalls and with a serious expression on his face. He lived only a short distance from the barbershop and told Holbrook that he was eminently contented with life in Home. "I have had forty years of as happy a life as man can know, and those forty years have proved to my satisfaction that Home colony was the right idea. But I have not now, any more than I ever have had, a desire to convert anybody to any particular belief or way of living, except by my own example. What is needed in this world is more pure reason."[20] With this last statement, the last remaining founder of Home betrayed that he still had a utopian streak in him.

"The stuff we printed in *Discontent* wouldn't raise an eyebrow today," explained the former printer Charles Govan at age seventy. "Law doesn't mean much. It's public opinion and not law that puts a man in jail for expressing his opinions on paper. The tragedy of public opinion is that it is always trailing along in the rear of reasonably progressive thinking. Thus, somebody is always the goat for any progressive step made by society."[21]

Home appeared to thrive in the 1930s, drawing significant revenue from its successful egg-candling business. A new community hall had replaced Liberty Hall, but instead of being collectively owned, it was a private enterprise. Members had to pay $12.50 to join the Peninsula Social Club. Dances and socials were held in the main room, and an eclectic and well-stocked library contained over two thousand volumes. Home was like any other rural community, according to Holbrook, except that the residents were conversant on the topics in those books.

As the century progressed, however, fewer and fewer of the original members appeared in the human-interest stories. Only six years later, in 1943, a reporter from a Tacoma newspaper encountered Jay Fox, now mostly bald. "The years and times may have tempered the ideas of this former publisher, for there is little of the radical apparent today as he works among his flowers and vines overlooking quiet, blue Joe's Bay," the article commented. "His old press is no more and a small press on which dodgers were printed, reposes in venerable rust in the garage."[22] Fox pointed out to the reporter, though, that many of the changes he'd advocated—an eight-hour work day, adequate compensation for workers, a free press, free speech, and women's rights—had all come to pass, and he expected that, with the end of the war, there would be an adjustment to better living conditions for all.

When Stewart Holbrook returned in 1946, writing this time for *The American Scholar*, he called again upon Jay Fox. Fox had always praised the beauty of a general strike, when the smoke of industry cleared and the blue skies stretched above. Perhaps he'd found a piece of this stillness on the edge of Joe's Bay, in the house he'd built with his own hands. Its proximity to the rhythms of the tides had gradually worn the edges of his fervor but had not snuffed out his ideals. "The fires of Revolution still burn in the old anarchist, perhaps the last of his kind, and he is happy when William Z. Foster, more in direct touch with the world, comes to visit him, as he does occasionally, and tells him how goes the battle with the minions of Capital."[23]

After one of these visits, at Foster's urging, Fox began writing his memoirs. Fox would pause and gaze out at the waters, attempting to gather up the patchwork of his life, and through his seventies he stitched much of his early life together, but when he turned eighty-one, he discovered the fabric had frayed too much. Fox died in 1961, before completing the project. His ashes were scattered on his property, and when the rains came, they washed the dust of Jay Fox into Puget Sound and the tides carried it to the ocean beyond.

)O(O(

"WE HAD UTOPIA," Evelyn says. The room has dimmed and we've turned on the lights. As we talk, the distance between us begins to fill up with her memories. I've stopped taking notes and I'm just basking in the glow of her remembrance. "We felt free and didn't have any fears. Nobody dreamed of anyone harming anybody. There weren't bad people around. It was a general feeling, not just in Home but on the Peninsula."

"When did it change?" I ask. People her children's age have told me about what it was like on the Peninsula in the 1970s. "It was like the Wild West out here," they've said and told stories of hard drugs, of buddies caught in gunfights while selling salmon in a parking lot. But I'm curious how she saw those days.

"I can't say. I was gone so long," she replies, referring to the years she lived away from Home.

Perhaps utopia is always an island, whether it lies somewhere in the future or in the past, and the distance throws certain qualities into relief. As we continue to talk, the orbit of her memories draws up a boy she knew in college, "a friend," she calls him, insisting: "I didn't date." They couldn't afford to date, so they went swimming at Green Lake in Seattle, things like that. He always told her he had a sweetheart in Mount Vernon or someplace north. His name was Kenyon, or Ken. Let's just call him Ken. "Oh, I don't know why I'm telling you this. This shouldn't go in your book."

"It won't if it doesn't have to do with Home," I say. But as she describes how she later visited Ken, who was stationed in San Francisco, and toured the big city, I realize she is telling me something about Home. She stayed with a family friend from Home, and over three days, Ken showed her the sights, took her to a fancy restaurant, and then she returned to Seattle.

"Nothing came of it," she says. "We weren't really interested in each other in that way. Later he sent me a letter saying that he'd married his childhood sweetheart. I appreciated that. I never heard from him again."

But there seems to be more to this story. Something was humming between these two young people, and Ken seems an emblem of what might have been different in her life, a time when she briefly entertained another trajectory, one that would have taken her away from the man she would eventually marry, as well as her children and grandchildren. Her little story draws up a mystery that lies at the heart of all history: when certain moments seem ripe with potential, why do things happen the way they do? In the clarity of hindsight, events appear inevitable or regretful or uncanny or any other interpretation that can be layered on to them. But in the midst of it, a young couple floats on a warm day in Green Lake, sun warming their shoulders, feet dangling in the water.

As I get up to leave and walk toward the door, Evelyn says, "I miss having a man around to talk to. My husband has been gone since 2002."

"I'm glad I could be that man for a couple of hours."

"Tallyho!" She calls as I descend the hill into the darkness.

Tonight a full moon illuminates the backs of the clouds so brilliantly that it looks as if a dark filter has been placed over a bright sky to give the illusion of night. Light shines through the tattered edges of the clouds much as the pebbles were visible through the translucent fringe of the jellyfish on shore. No star can be seen anywhere above.

Walking on A Street toward my car, I pass houses that look like any other in the night. A huge window brightly displays the interior of a newer one, large and colonial style: big brown couches, granite counter tops, frenetic images playing across a flat screen TV, a woman with her hands in a sink. Down the road, I see the Retherfords' A-frame home completely dark, and in the cone of light beneath a street lamp, the mound of grass over the dinghy.

I get in my car and drive slowly down the street. As I approach the intersection, my headlights pan across two teenagers sitting on the metal guardrail. They emerge briefly—a male and a female, slouched and bored-looking, waiting for something to happen—and then they disappear back into the gloom. I want to stop, ask them what it's like to grow up in Home today, but then I think of Padgum living with Jay and Cora Fox. Much will remain in Home that I will never know.

At the blinking red light of the Key Peninsula Highway, I look both ways up and down the road, and seeing the way clear, I turn right and begin the drive back to my own home.

ACKNOWLEDGEMENTS

Writing a book is something of a utopian endeavor, and this one is stronger for the many hands that participated in its making. The idea to write about Home originated in a conversation I had with Brian Kenney over five years ago. Since then, Brian exerted not only a strong, indirect influence on the course of this book, but our circle of friends has made Tacoma feel like home.

A significant portion of *Trying Home* was completed while attending the Rainier Writing Workshop at Pacific Lutheran University. My mentors Rebecca McClanahan, Sherry Simpson, and Mary Blew offered guidance and encouragement while I learned how to tell the story of Home. I must thank Stan Rubin and Judith Kitchen for creating an environment where my writing could flourish. Finally, the members of the 2011 nonfiction cohort (a.k.a. 2 Matches) provided insightful responses and suggestions to the manuscript, as well as the prodding and emotional support to sustain the work after graduation.

Trying Home would not have been possible without the research of others, especially Charles LeWarne, Gregory Hall, and Sylvia Retherford. Many others played important roles in my direct research into the place of Home. David Spencer drove me there in his boat. Lisa Johnson lent me a camera to duplicate a number of images that appear in this book. Dale Goodwin introduced me to Lorraine Hart, who in turn shared with me what it was like to live in Home. Colleen Slater discussed the history of Home and connected me to local residents. Evelyn Evans kindly spent an evening sharing her memories of growing up in Home.

This book was first conceived in and then thrived as a result of libraries and librarians. I benefited from the materials on Home at the University of Washington Libraries, the Key Peninsula Historical Society, the Tacoma Public Library Northwest Room, the Washington State Historical Society, and Gonzaga University Library. Several librarians were pivotal to this work. Glenda Pearson and Jessica Albano employed me as a graduate student in "MicNews" and then roped me into the project where I first came across *The Agitator*. Jean Fisher at the Tacoma Public Library Northwest Room helped me track down sources I could not find on my own. Charles Lord, the Director of the University of Washington Tacoma Library (and my supervisor), suggested and then authorized the use of a time grant for me to finish this book.

Karolina Waclawiak at *The Believer* offered valuable suggestions on "The Anarchists Must Go," which was published in a slightly different version in the magazine's March/April 2013 issue.

Finally, I am deeply indebted to the family with whom I have shared a sense of home, from my parents, who first taught me what home was, to my two sons, who continue to teach me the hard and joyful lessons of how to create a home. I am especially grateful for my wife Emily who recognized my abilities to write true stories before I did. She has spent countless hours over the past five years listening to my struggles with this book, editing various versions of the manuscript, and releasing me briefly from my fatherly duties to research and write. This book would not exist without her.

SELECTED BIBLIOGRAPHY:
SOURCES ON HOME AND ITS RESIDENTS

Balzer, Anitra. "Donald Vose: A Homegrown Traitor." *Communal Societies* 8 (December 1988): 90-103.

Gaskine, J. W. "The Anarchists of Home." *The Independent*, Apr. 28, 1910: 914-22.

Hall, Gregory David. *The Theory and Practice of Anarchism at Home Colony, 1896-1912.* Thesis (M.A.)—Washington State University, 1994.

Holbrook, Stewart H. "Home Sweet Home." *The Oregonian*, Dec. 5, 12, and 21, 1937.

———. "Anarchists at Home." *American Scholar* 15 (Autumn 1946): 425-38.

———. "Brook Farm, Wild West Style." *American Mercury* 57 (August 1943): 216-23.

Sreenivasan, Jyotsna. "Home" in *Utopias in American History*. Santa Barbara, Calif: ABC-CLIO, 2008: 165-69.

Hong, Nathaniel. "Free Speech without an 'if' or a 'but': The Defense of Free Expression in the Radical Periodicals of Home, Washington, 1897-1912." *American Journalism* 11, no. 2 (1994): 139-53.

Koenig, Brigitte. "Law and Disorder at Home: Free Love, Free Speech, and the Search for an Anarchist Utopia." *Labor History* 45, no. 2 (2004): 199-223.

LeWarne, Charles Pierce. *Utopias on Puget Sound, 1885-1915.* Seattle: University of Washington Press, 1995.

Morgan, Murray. *The Last Wilderness.* Seattle: University of Washington Press, 1976.

Retherford, Sylvia. *Home at Home.* [Tacoma, Wash.]: All My Somedays, 1982.

Retherford, Sylvia. *Compilation of Writings and Photos Concerned with the History of Home, Washington.* [Assembled in 1985 for the Key Center Branch of Pierce County Library.]

CITED SOURCES

INTRODUCTION

1 Fox, Jay, Papers, University of Washington Libraries Special Collections.
2 Fox, Jay, "Greetings to You All," *The Agitator*, Nov. 15, 1910.
3 LeWarne, Charles Pierce, *Utopias on Puget Sound, 1885-1915* (Seattle: University of Washington Press, 1995), 220.

CHAPTER ONE: THE MOTHER OF PROGRESS FINDS HOME

1 Kipling, Rudyard, *From Sea to Sea; Letters of Travel* (New York: Doubleday & McClure Company, 1899), 43.
2 Allen, George, "Inside Workings of Anarchistic Colony Revealed," *The Tacoma Daily Ledger,* Jan. 7, 1912.
3 Meany, Edmond S., *Vancouver's Discovery of Puget Sound: Portraits and Biographies of the Men Honored in the Naming of Geographic Features of Northwestern America* (New York: Macmillan, 1907), 155.
4 Gaskine, J. W., "The Anarchists of Home," *The Independent*, Apr. 28, 1910, 916.
5 Bellamy, Edward, *Looking Backward, 2000-1887* (Reprint, New York: Penguin Books, 1982), 203.
6 Franklin, John, "Edward Bellamy and Nationalism," *The New England Quarterly* 11 no. 4 (1938): 754.
7 "Washington Colony of Anarchists," *The Tacoma Daily Ledger,* Feb. 26, 1898.
8 Retherford, Sylvia, *Home at Home* (Tacoma: All My Somedays, 1982), 12-13.
9 Gaskine, 916.
10 Allen.
11 "Washington Colony of Anarchists."
12 Nell, Painter, *Standing at Armageddon, 1877-1919* (New York: Norton, 2008), xvi.
13 Gaskine, 916.
14 Retherford, 8.
15 Ibid., 14.
16 Retherford, Sylvia, "Why Our Villages Are So Named," in *Compilation of Writings and Photos Concerned with the History of Home*, Northwest Room, Tacoma Public Library.
17 Retherford, *Home at Home*, 31-32.
18 Allen.
19 "Wanted," *New Era*, March 1897. Copy in Retherford, *Compilation*.
20 "Washington Colony of Anarchists."
21 Ibid.

22 Ibid.

23 Kropotkin, Peter, "Anarchism," in *The Encyclopædia Britannica: A Dictionary of Arts, Sciences, Literature and General Information*, ed. Hugh Chisholm (Cambridge, England: at the university press, 1910), 914.

24 Ibid.

25 Ibid.

26 Hunter, Robert, *The American Encyclopædic Dictionary: A Most Complete and Thoroughly Modern Dictionary of the English Language* (Chicago: W. B. Conkey Co., 1895), 180.

27 My analysis and depiction of the image is based upon Green, James R., *Death in the Haymarket: A Story of Chicago, the First Labor Movement, and the Bombing That Divided Gilded Age America* (New York: Pantheon Books, 2006), 206-7.

28 Quote from Merriman, John M., *The Dynamite Club: How a Bombing in Fin-De-Siècle Paris Ignited the Age of Modern Terror* (Boston: Houghton Mifflin Harcourt, 2009), 63.

29 Tuchman, Barbara, *The Proud Tower: A Portrait of the World before the War, 1890-1914* (New York: Macmillan, 1966), 63-113.

30 Berkman, Alexander, *Prison Memoirs of an Anarchist* (Reprint, New York: New York Review of Books, 1999), 11-12.

31 Gaskine, 918.

32 Warner, Charles Dudley, "Thoughts Suggested By Mr. Froude's 'Progress,'" in *The Complete Writings of Charles Dudley Warner, vol. 15.* (Hartford, Conn: American Pub. Co., 1904), 195-96.

33 "Greetings," *Discontent*, May 11, 1898.

34 Cowell, F. A., "Ideas and Criticisms," *Discontent*, May 18, 1898.

35 Miles, Elum, "Problem Solved," *Discontent*, May 11, 1898.

36 Penhallow, Charles, "Joe's Bay," *Discontent*, May 18, 1898.

37 Verity, Oliver, "Do You Want a Home?" *Discontent*, May 18, 1898.

38 Allen, George, "Freedom, the Natural Remedy," *Discontent*, May 25, 1898.

39 "Association Notes," *Discontent*, July 13, 1898.

40 "Association Notes," *Discontent*, July 20, 1898.

41 "Association Notes," *Discontent*, Aug. 24, 1898.

42 "Association Notes," *Discontent*, July 13, 1898.

43 "Association Notes," *Discontent*, Oct. 26, 1898.

44 "Association Notes," *Discontent*, July 20, 1898.

45 "Association Notes," *Discontent*, Oct. 12, 1898.

46 Avrich, Paul, *Anarchist Voices: An Oral History of Anarchism in America* (Princeton, N.J: Princeton University Press, 1995), 292.

47 "Association Notes," *Discontent*, Oct. 26, 1898.

48 LeWarne, Charles P., *Utopias on Puget Sound, 1885-1915* (Seattle: University of Washington Press, 1995), 173.

49 "Association Notes," *Discontent*, Jan. 11, 1899.
50 Ibid.

LIFE AT HOME: SHELTER

1 LaVene, Radium, "There Was No Place Like Home," (unpublished manuscript, Sept. 25, 1945), Key Peninsula Historical Society, 13.
2 Ibid., 12.
3 Slater, Colleen A., *The Key Peninsula* (Charleston, SC: Arcadia Pub, 2007), 32.
4 Verity, Oliver, "Do You Want a Home," *Discontent*, May 18, 1898.
5 Snyder Hartung Kane Strauss Architects, *Home, Washington Historic District: Survey and Inventory*, n.d., submitted to Pierce County Historic Preservation Program. Copies available from the Pierce County Library System.
6 There was no publication in Home in 1908 to provide a precise number. These statistics come from a count two years later included in "Home," *The Agitator*, Nov. 15, 1910.
7 LaVene, 12.

CHAPTER TWO: THE ANARCHISTS MUST GO

1 "Association Notes," *Discontent*, Sept. 11, 1901.
2 Quote from Passet, Joanne, "Power through Print: Lois Waisbrooker and Grassroots Feminism," in *Women in Print: Essays on the Print Culture of American Women from the Nineteenth and Twentieth Centuries*, eds. Danky, James and Wayne Wiegand (Madison: University of Wisconsin Press, 2006), 241.
3 Adams, James, "Hear the Other Side," *Discontent*, Sept. 11, 1901.
4 LeWarne, Charles. "The Anarchist Colony at Home, Washington, 1901-1902," *Arizona and the West*, 14 no. 2 (1972): 160.
5 "Nation's Ruler Shot by Anarchist," *The Tacoma Daily Ledger*, Sept. 7, 1901.
6 Ibid.
7 "No Sympathy for a Traitor," *The Tacoma Daily Ledger*, Sept. 7, 1901.
8 "A Hint of Mob Law," *The Tacoma Daily Ledger*, Sept. 7, 1901.
9 "Text of Assassin's Confession," *The Tacoma Daily Ledger*, Sept. 8, 1901.
10 Quote from Rauchway, Eric, *Murdering McKinley: The Making of Theodore Roosevelt's America* (New York: Hill and Wang, 2003), 102.
11 "Emma Goldman Is Arrested," *Tacoma Evening News*, Sept. 10, 1901.
12 "Exterminate the Anarchists," *The Tacoma Daily Ledger*, Sept. 9, 1901.
13 "Warnings Sounded from the Pulpits," *The Tacoma Daily Ledger*, Sept. 9, 1901.
14 "Search Light on 'Home' Group," *Tacoma Evening News*, Sept. 12, 1901.
15 "The Outlaws of Home," *The Tacoma Daily Ledger*, Sept. 14, 1901.
16 "Anarchy Must Be Stamped Out," *The Tacoma Daily Ledger*, Sept. 15, 1901.
17 "To Fight Anarchy," *The Tacoma Daily Ledger*, Sept. 17, 1901.

18 Retherford, Sylvia, *Home at Home* (Tacoma: All My Somedays, 1982), 36.

19 Verity, Oliver, "Something about Discontent," *Discontent*, Nov. 20, 1902.

20 "Minister Visits the Home Colony," *The Tacoma Daily Ledger*, Sept. 30, 1901.

21 "Leaders Arrested," *The Tacoma Daily Ledger*, Sept. 25, 1901.

22 Ibid.

23 Ibid.

24 Goldman, Emma, "The Tragedy at Buffalo," *Free Society*, Oct. 6, 1901.

25 Morton, James F., Jr., "To the Liberal Public," *Discontent*, Nov. 13, 1901.

26 Morton, James F., Jr., "Discontent Held Up!" *Discontent*, Dec. 18, 1901.

27 "Home to Lose Post Office," *The Tacoma Daily Ledger*, March 8, 1902.

28 "The Federal Grand Jury and the Home Post Office," *The Tacoma Daily Ledger*, March 10, 1902.

29 Morton, James F., Jr., "Victory!" *Discontent*, March 19, 1902.

30 Adams, James, "A Healthy Comparison," *Discontent*, January 30, 1901.

31 Trial described in "Anarchist Cases Are Thrown Out," *Tacoma Evening News*, March 11, 1902.

32 Morton, "Victory!"

33 Hughes, Charles Hamilton, "Medical Aspects of the Czolgosz Case," *Alienist and Neurologist: A Quarterly Journal of Scientific, Clinical and Forensic Psychiatry and Neurology*, 23 no. 1 (1902): 42.

34 Morton, James F., Jr., "Czolgosz Was Insane," *Discontent*, March 19, 1902.

35 Morton, James F., Jr., "A New Infamy," *Discontent*, April 23, 1902.

36 "Editress is Found Guilty," *The Tacoma Daily Ledger*, July 16, 1902.

37 Cartoon included in Retherford, Sylvia, *Compilation of Writings and Photos Concerned with the History of Home*, Northwest Room, Tacoma Public Library.

38 LeWarne, Charles P. *Utopias on Puget Sound, 1885-1915*, 185-6.

39 Morton, James F., Jr., "Freedom of Expression," *The Demonstrator*, March 11, 1903.

LIFE AT HOME: WORK

1 Vose, Gertie, "A Letter," *Demonstrator*, March 16, 1904.

2 "Home News," *Demonstrator*, June 17, 1903.

3 Retherford, Sylvia. "Early Business in Home," in *Compilation of Writings and Photos Concerned with the History of Home*, Northwest Room, Tacoma Public Library.

4 "Home News," *Demonstrator*, March 16, 1904.

CHAPTER THREE: NO SPIRES, NO SALOONS

1 Diary can be found in Muirhead, Eugene, Papers, 1900-1912, Microfilm # A1991, University of Washington Libraries Microforms/Newspaper Collection. Subsequent quotations by Muirhead also from his diary.

2   Van Buskirk, Philip, Diaries 1851-1902, University of Washington Libraries Special Collections.

3   Van Buskirk, Philip, and Robert D. Monroe, *Sailor on the Snohomish*, Microfilm # A799, University of Washington Libraries Microforms/ Newspaper Collection.

4   Van Buskirk, Diaries. Subsequent quotations by Van Buskirk also from his diaries.

5   Lang, Lucy R., *Tomorrow Is Beautiful* (New York: Macmillan, 1948), 48. Subsequent quotations by Lang also from this memoir. Also, during the time period portrayed here Lang would have been known by her married name "Lucy Robins." She and Bob Robins later divorced in the 1920s, and soon afterward, she married Harry Lang and took his last name. To avoid confusion regarding quotes from this memoir, I have used her name at the time of writing it.

6   Webster, Noah, and Noah Porter, *Webster's Revised Unabridged Dictionary* (Springfield: G. & C. Merriam Co, 1913). Available via *The ARTFL Project* at the University of Chicago: http://machaut.uchicago.edu/websters.

7   Lang, 51.

8   Burns, William J., *The Masked War: The Story of a Peril That Threatened the United States* (New York: George H. Doran Co, 1913), 69.

9   Lang, 52.

10 Burns, 23. Subsequent quotations from Burns also from this memoir.

11 Holbrook, Stewart, "Home Sweet Home: The Anarchists of Joe's Bay," *The Oregonian*, December 19, 1937.

12 Burns, *Masked War*, 89-91.

LIFE AT HOME: LEISURE

1   LaVene, Radium, "There Was No Place Like Home," (unpublished manuscript, Sept. 25, 1945), Key Peninsula Historical Society, 8.

2   "Home News," *The Demonstrator*, Feb. 21, 1906.

3   Morton, James F., Jr., "Demonstrative," *The Demonstrator*, April 22, 1903.

4   Hubbard, Elbert, "Heart to Heart Talks with Philistines from the Pastor to His Flock," *The Philistine*, 18 no. 3 (Feb. 1904), 81-82.

5   Professor Thompson's visit is described in LaVene, Radium, "There Was No Place like Home"; Jay Fox's unfinished memoir in his papers in the Gonzaga University Library Special Collections; and Holbrook, Stewart, "Home Sweet Home," *The Oregonian*, Dec. 12, 1937.

CHAPTER FOUR: CROWNING AN AGITATOR

1   "Home," *The Agitator*, Nov. 15, 1910.

2   Hapgood, Hutchins, *The Spirit of Labor*, ed. James R. Barrett (Reprint, Urbana: University of Illinois Press, 2004), 286.

3   Ibid, 290.

4 "Comrades and Friends," *The Agitator*, Nov. 15, 1910.

5 Fox, Jay, "The Nude and the Prudes," *The Agitator*, July 1, 1911.

6 Lang, Lucy R., *Tomorrow Is Beautiful* (New York: Macmillan, 1948), 49.

7 Fox, Jay, "The Chicago Martyrs," *The Agitator*, Nov. 15, 1910.

8 Ibid.

9 All quotes from: "Women Guilty of Nude Bathing," *The Tacoma Daily Ledger*, July 23, 1911.

10 Fox, Jay, "Arrest of the Editor," *The Agitator*, Sept. 1, 1911.

11 *Remington & Ballinger's Annotated Codes and Statutes of Washington Showing All Statutes in Force: Including the Extraordinary Session Laws of 1909* (Seattle: Bancroft-Whitney Company, 1910), §2564. The law in full states: "Every person who shall willfully print, publish, edit, issue, or knowingly circulate, sell, distribute or display any book, paper, document, or written or printed matter, in any form, advocating, encouraging or inciting, or having a tendency to encourage or incite the commission of any crime, breach of the peace, or act of violence, or which shall tend to encourage or advocate disrespect for law or for any court or courts of justice, shall be guilty of a gross misdemeanor."

12 "Jay Fox, Editor of Agitator Is Placed in Jail," *Tacoma Daily Tribune*, Aug. 24, 1911.

13 "Hung Jury in Joe's Bay Bathing Case," *Tacoma Daily Tribune*, Aug. 25, 1911.

14 "Fined Heavily for Almost Nude Swim," *The Tacoma Daily Ledger*, Aug. 26, 1911.

15 "Statement of Facts," State of Washington v. Jay Fox, No. 10451, Washington State Supreme Court, Nov. 1912.

16 Fox, Jay, "Home and Its Traducers," *The Agitator*, Aug. 15, 1911 ; Koenig, Brigitte, "Law and Disorder at Home: Free Love, Free Speech, and the Search for an Anarchist Utopia," *Labor History*, 45 no. 2 (2004): 215.

17 LeWarne, Charles P, *Utopias on Puget Sound, 1885-1915* (Seattle: University of Washington Press, 1995), 214.

18 "Statement of Facts," State of Washington v. Jay Fox, No. 10451, Washington State Supreme Court, Nov. 1912.

19 "Reach No Verdict After Fox Pleads," *The Tacoma Daily Ledger*, Jan. 12, 1912.

20 "Jury Has Long Debate Over Fate of Editor," *The Tacoma Times*, Jan 12, 1912; "Editor Found Guilty," *The Agitator*, Jan. 15, 1912; and Morgan, Murray, *The Last Wilderness*, (Seattle: University of Washington Press, 1976), 119.

21 "Find Fox Guilty," *Tacoma Daily Ledger*, Jan. 13, 1912.

22 "Tillman of Home Colony Hands Star to Sheriff," *Tacoma Daily Tribune*, Jan. 15, 1912.

23 "Nude Bathing Drew Large Audience," *The Tacoma Times*, Jan. 17, 1912.

24 LaVene, Radium, "There Was No Place Like Home," (unpublished manuscript, Sept. 25, 1945), Key Peninsula Historical Society: 24.

25 Fox, Jay, "The Agitator in History: I," *The Agitator*, Feb. 15, 1912.

26 Fox, Jay, "The Agitator in History: II," *The Agitator*, March 1, 1912.

27 Fox, Jay, "The Agitator in History: III," *The Agitator*, March 15, 1912.

28 Fox, Jay, "The Agitator in History: VI," *The Agitator*, Apr. 1, 1912.

29 Quote from Johanningsmeier, Edward P., *Forging American Communism: The Life of William Z. Foster* (Princeton: Princeton University Press, 1994), 58.

30 Lang, 49.

31 Berkman, Alexander, *Prison Memoirs of an Anarchist* (Reprint, New York: New York Review of Books, 1999), 505.

32 Schroeder, Theodore, *Free Speech Case of Jay Fox* (New York: Free Speech League, 1912), 5.

33 Carr, Mary M., "Jay Fox: Anarchist of Home," *Columbia* Magazine 4 no. 1 (Spring 1990): 8.

34 Fox v. State of Washington, 236 U.S. 273 (1915).

35 United States v. Schwimmer, 279 U.S. 644 (1929).

36 Verity's and Muirhead's letters included with Muirhead, Eugene. Papers, 1900-1912. Microfilm # A1991. Microforms/Newspaper Collection, U of Washington Libraries, Seattle, Washington. Print.

37 "Jay Fox of Nude Fame Starts Sentence," *Tacoma Daily Tribune*, July 27, 1915.

LIFE AT HOME: EDUCATION

1 Allen, George, "A Comparison," *Discontent*, Nov. 28, 1900.

2 Muirhead, Eugene, Papers, 1900-1912, Microfilm # A1991, University of Washington Libraries Microforms/Newspaper Collection.

3 Note included in image from University of Washington Digital Collections http://content.lib.washington.edu/cdm4/item_viewer.php?CISOROOT=/social&CISOPTR=95

4 "Some Disadvantages of Anarchism," *The Independent*, Dec. 25, 1905: 3103-4.

5 Eyges, T., "My Visit to Home," *The Demonstrator*, Sept. 4, 1907.

6 "Home Life," *The Agitator*, Jan. 1, 1911.

7 Harrison, J.C., "One Picture of 'Home Colony,'" *Solidarity*, Feb. 13, 1915.

8 Travaglio, Eugene, "Trials of a Noble Experiment," (unpublished manuscript, 1966), Washington State Historical Society, 7.

9 LaVene, Radium, "There Was No Place Like Home," (unpublished manuscript, Sept. 25, 1945), Key Peninsula Historical Society, 26.

CHAPTER FIVE: HOW CAIN DIES

1   Goldman, Emma, *Living My Life* (Garden City: Garden City Pub. Co, 1934), 556.

2   "Beaten by Anarchists, Donald Meserve Flees to Boat to Save Life," *Seattle Times*, Jan. 28, 1916. During this period in his life, Vose began identifying himself as "Donald Meserve," using his father's last name instead of his mother's. I suspect he did this to distance himself from his mother and his past. For the sake of consistency, I chosen to use "Vose," the name he was known by among the anarchists. More about his name can be found in Anitra Balzar's article about Vose cited below, 90-91.

3   LeWarne, Charles, "Children of Home," included in Retherford, Sylvia, *Compilation of Writings and Photos Concerned with the History of Home*, Northwest Room, Tacoma Public Library.

4   LaVene, Radium, "There Was No Place Like Home," (unpublished manuscript, Sept. 25, 1945), Key Peninsula Historical Society.

5   LeWarne, "Children of Home."

6   Balzar, Anitra, "Donald Vose: A Home Grown Traitor," *Communal Societies* 8 (1988): 97.

7   This summary draws on: Adamic, Louis, *Dynamite: The Story of Class Violence in America* (New York: Viking Press, 1934), 189-242; Gottlieb, Robert, and Irene Wolt, *Thinking Big: The Story of the Los Angeles Times, Its Publishers, and Their Influence on Southern California* (New York: Putnam, 1977), 82-105; and Noel, James, "The Great Dynamite Conspiracy," *Los Angeles Times*, Oct. 1, 1933.

8   Burns, William J., *The Masked War: The Story of a Peril That Threatened the United States* (New York: George H. Doran Co, 1913), 326.

9   Lang, Lucy R., *Tomorrow Is Beautiful* (New York: Macmillan, 1948), 80.

10 "Marked Man Bares 'Red' Plots – Anarchist Moves Are Revealed," *Seattle Times*, May 22, 1916.

11 Quote from Balzar, 93.

12 O'Neill, Eugene, *The Iceman Cometh* (New Haven: Yale University Press, 2006), 32.

13 "Meserve Tells of His Meeting with Caplan," *Seattle Times*, May 23, 1916.

14 Goldman, Emma, "Donald Vose: The Accursed," in Glassgold, Peter, *Anarchy!: An Anthology of Emma Goldman's Mother Earth* (Washington, D.C: Counterpoint, 2001), 349. Subsequent quotations by Goldman are from the same source.

15 Hapgood, Hutchins, *An Anarchist Woman* (New York: Duffield & Co, 1909), 19.

16 Goldman, "Donald Vose: The Accursed," 350.

17 "Marked Man Bares 'Red' Plots – Anarchist Moves Are Revealed."

18 Ibid.

19 This depiction of life with Terry Carlin comes from Gelb, Arthur, and Barbara Gelb, *O'Neill* (New York: Harper & Row, 1974), 284-86.

20 "Marked Man Bares 'Red' Plots – Anarchist Moves Are Revealed."

21 O'Neill, 136-37.

22 Lang, 77-83.

23 "Intimidation Attempted," *Los Angeles Times,* Nov. 19, 1915.

24 "Says Schmidt Boasted of Deed," *New York Times,* Dec. 21, 1915.

25 "Defense Loses at Every Turn," *Los Angeles Times,* Dec. 23, 1915.

26 Goldman, "Donald Vose: The Accursed," 351.

27 "Dynamite Case to be Retried," *Los Angeles Times,* May 17, 1916.

28 "Marked Man Bares 'Red' Plots – Anarchist Moves Are Revealed."

29 Goldman, "Donald Vose: The Accursed," 351.

30 Balzar, 96.

31 LaVene; and Avrich, Paul, *Anarchist Voices: An Oral History of Anarchism in America* (Oakland: AK Press, 2005), 295.

32 O'Neill, 203.

33 Gelb, 282-94; and Alexander, Doris, *Eugene O'Neill's Last Plays: Separating Art from Autobiography* (Athens: University of Georgia Press, 2005), 29-44.

34 O'Neill, 217.

LIFE AT HOME: TRANSPORTATION

1 This example of a small-scale maritime disaster, as well the stories that precede it, come from LaVene, Radium, "There Was No Place Like Home" (unpublished manuscript, Sept. 25, 1945), Key Peninsula Historical Society.

CHAPTER SIX: UTOPIA CORRUPTED

1 "Home Colony Utopia About to Collapse," *The Tacoma Times,* Dec. 7, 1918.

2 Oscar Engvall … vs. Ann Haiman …, Civil File 43388, Pierce County Superior Court.

3 "Burglary Case in Jury's Hand," *Tacoma Times,* Jan. 13, 1909.

4 "Communistic Land Holding Abandoned," *Tacoma Daily Ledger,* June 27, 1909.

5 "Home Colony in Court," *Tacoma Daily Ledger,* April 7, 1912.

6 "Corruption in 'Utopia' Near Tacoma Charged," *Tacoma Daily News,* Aug. 23, 1916.

7 "Home's Tangled Affairs," *Tacoma Times,* Jan. 18, 1917.

8 Harrison, J.C., "One Picture of 'Home Colony," *Solidarity,* February 13, 1915.

9 Holbrook, Stewart, "Home Sweet Home: The Anarchists of Joe's Bay," *The Oregonian,* Dec. 19, 1937.

10 Civil File 43388.

11 Letter can be found in Muirhead, Eugene, Papers, 1900-1912, Microfilm # A1991, University of Washington Libraries Microforms/Newspaper Collection.

12 Civil File 43388.

13 Ibid.

14 Snyder Hartung Kane Strauss Architects, *Home, Washington Historic District: Survey and Inventory*, n.d., submitted to Pierce County Historic Preservation Program. Copies available from the Pierce County Library System.

15 Civil File 43388.

16 Kanter, Rosabeth M., *Commitment and Community: Communes and Utopias in Sociological Perspective* (Cambridge, Mass: Harvard University Press, 1972), 64.

17 Kanter, 102.

18 Slosson, E. E., "An Experiment in Anarchy," *Independent*, April 2, 1903: 784.

19 Holbrook, Stewart, "Home Sweet Home: The Anarchists of Joe's Bay," *The Oregonian*, Dec. 19, 1937.

20 Ibid.

21 Ibid.

22 "Only Memories Remain of Home Colony's Past," *Tacoma Ledger-News Tribune*, Aug. 29, 1943.

23 Holbrook, Stewart, "The Anarchists at Home," *The American Scholar*, 15 (Autumn 1946): 438.

INDEX